In Praise of
Living with a Grieving Heart

Marianne Bette has suffered several very significant losses during her life. In her book, *Living with a Grieving Heart*, Marianne shares her experiences and insights regarding the painful grieving process. She writes about her own, often debilitating, reactions to loss in a very honest and candid manner, offering suggestions for working through these difficult times. Through her stories, the reader will come to realize that many of the emotions the bereaved experiences, including deep despair and cognitive changes, are natural and normal. While grieving is very difficult and painful, Marianne shows the bereaved that they can grow from the experience of loss, incorporating the loss into their future, and finding positive ways to put together a life that may be different, but meaningful.

— **Carol Flament, MS,** Death, Dying and Bereavement Educator
and Bereavement Support Group Facilitator

As a doctor who treats chronic pain patients, I have had the rare opportunity to witness the transformation of suffering into joyful triumph—an evolution that eludes many. I deeply admire those who can convert adversity into a positive force. For those who are heart-broken and need help, Dr. Marianne Bette provides a prescription for transformation. In *Living with a Grieving Heart*, she allows us to glimpse her own grief as illustrated in a series of honest, powerful and sometimes raw anecdotes. She inspires us to embrace the complexities of grief and use the transformative power of anguish to deepen relationships and generate new enthusiasm for life. Marianne possesses a level of wisdom that could only have been earned by enduring incredible heartache. She inspires her readers with her extraordinary insight and gift of resilience. Marianne's message is clear. The Paradox of Life always hides blessings in our hardships.

— **Jim Prado, DC,** Chiropractic Physician

In her latest book, Marianne Bette again offers us important insights for living and an intimate portrait of pivotal moments in her life journey. The stories are offset by words of wisdom, encouragement and perspective in dealing with grief born of loss. Marianne's book deals with the loss of a loved one. What happens when that loved one is yourself? Many people who suffer a brain injury experience the grief of losing the life they knew and the future they anticipated. They and their families will find comfort and guidance in these pages as they forge ahead in their life journeys. Grief is universal; only the details vary.

— **Kathleen M. Lord, MS,** Speech-Language Pathologist

Living
WITH A
GRIEVING HEART

Other Books by the Author
Living with a Dead Man

Living
WITH A
GRIEVING HEART

Thoughts of Gratitude
from a Grief Warrior

Marianne Bette, MD

EMERALD LAKE
BOOKS
Sherman, Connecticut

Books published by Emerald Lake Books may be ordered through your favorite booksellers or by visiting emeraldlakebooks.com.

Library of Congress Cataloging-in-Publication Data

Names: Bette, Marianne, author.

Title: Living with a grieving heart / Marianne Bette.

Description: [Sherman, Connecticut] : [Emerald Lake Books], [2022] |
   Summary: "Grief can make you crazy. It can shut you down, but grief can
   also crack you open and change you like nothing else. You can become
   your best self. If you let it, it can be the transformation of your
   lifetime. Dr. Marianne Bette shares stories from her own personal
   experiences with grief as well as from forty years in family medicine,
   to help those who are grieving learn how to embrace life again while
   living with a grieving heart"-- Provided by publisher.

Identifiers: LCCN 2022005774 (print) | LCCN 2022005775 (ebook) | ISBN
   9781945847585 (paperback) | ISBN 9781945847592 (epub)

Subjects: LCSH: Bette, Marianne. | Grief. | Bereaved persons--Anecdotes. |
   Women physicians--United States--Biography. | Widows--United
   States--Biography.

Classification: LCC BF575.G7 B4818 2022 (print) | LCC BF575.G7 (ebook) |
   DDC 155.9/37--dc23/eng/20220309

LC record available at https://lccn.loc.gov/2022005774

LC ebook record available at https://lccn.loc.gov/2022005775

To all grievers who carry on with gratitude.
And for Mario, our angel in disguise.

Contents

Part III. Trying to Be Normal

Part IV. Firsts Without

Part V. Moving On

Part VI. Kids and Grief

Excerpt from *Living with a Dead Man*

Introduction

*A*FTER I WROTE MY FIRST BOOK, *Living with a Dead Man*, about the last year of my husband's life, I thought my work was done. Many people told me how much that book helped them deal with or understand how to live with someone who has a terminal illness. Then, one day in my office, after a patient of mine thanked me for writing it, she looked me in the eye and said, "You have to write another."

Her statement shocked me. "You are kidding, right? That one nearly killed me," I replied.

"I hear you," she said. "But Dr. Bette, dying is easier than grieving. My mother died in three months, but it has been three years, and it's still really tough for me. Without her, my rock…" She had to clear her throat to continue. "You have to write a book on grief."

Oh my God, I thought. *She is right. Grief has no end*. We looked at each other—two people struck by a universal truth at the same time.

"Okay... I'll think about it." I tucked the idea away for safekeeping.

It's funny how some things just stay with you. In many ways, death is easier than living with grief.

Now, freshly retired after forty years of practicing family medicine, I am following through on the promise I made that day. These stories and insights about grief come from my doctoring and personal experiences. I hope they will soothe the pain of your grieving, help you understand how others grieve, and reveal the lessons death teaches us.

Grief can make you crazy. It can shut you down. But grief can also crack you open and change you like nothing else. You can become your best self. If you let it, grief can ignite the transformation of your lifetime. I hope some of these stories will convince you of this truth—the truth that grief warriors already know.

A warrior is defined as a person with a willingness to fight for what's right. I would add that a warrior is also a person who has fought in more than a few battles and has developed survival skills and strategies that allow her to lead others in battle. Together, they win wars.

And a *grief warrior* is a person who has been in the depths of despair and has battled overwhelming sorrow of loss with courage and strength of spirit. He has been victorious over darkness to win peace and understanding.

What I have learned from my battles as a grief warrior is that the wounds from losing loved ones contain beauty, power and courage. These experiences are precious, and their value as a way of understanding life is immeasurable. Grief has given me a reverence for life and love that I did not have before. I now know that love can transcend time, space and consciousness. It is a circle with no end. Love does not stop at death. It continues on and is almighty.

I hope these stories can impart that warrior spirit to you, so you can tuck that grief under your wing and fly to the heights, enjoying your life unburdened.

My Story

*A*FTER SIX YEARS OF COLLEGE, four years of medical school, and three intensive years of residency, graduation felt like getting out of jail. I had free time. I could do what I wanted when I wanted to (more or less) and enjoyed figuring out who I was when I wasn't studying, working in the hospital, or trying to catch up on sleep. Backpacking in the High Sierras with friends, playing racquetball several times a week, attending ground school, and taking flying lessons made the time zoom by. I worked one twenty-four-hour shift a week in an emergency room in the desert. I had the world by the tail.

That was when I met Kerry. He was the epitome of the tall, dark and handsome thirty-year-old, with blue eyes and a gorgeous beard. Kerry ran the heart-lung machine in the operating room during open heart surgery. He was also a pilot, racquetball star and part owner of a local bar.

Our professions, hobbies and interests were a match. We fell madly in love and spent every spare moment together. When Kerry and I got engaged, we flew back to Connecticut to celebrate with my family.

A few weeks later, he was selling his small, fast plane for a bigger one. While Kerry and the buyer were up in the plane, I was daydreaming about the trip we were taking to Los Angeles that afternoon to pick out our wedding rings. My dreaming soon turned nightmarish though, when Kerry's mechanic entered the waiting room; his face ashen. I knew with just one look that something awful must have happened. With our intense connection, I thought I would somehow sense our tearing apart when Kerry's plane crashed, but I never felt his death. Yet after that, I was never the same.

I have never written about my first experience with grief, losing Kerry, until now, where I've shared some of my feelings from after he died in this book.

Grief due to an accident, murder or suicide is what I refer to as "unexpected grief." No one sees it coming, least of all you. The person you love is there one moment, and then they are gone forever. Unexpected grief or sudden death is more traumatic than an expected death, and the grieving process often takes a lot longer, especially if you are young and have had no significant history with grief.

Even as a doctor, someone exposed to more death than an average person, I was unprepared for what I was about to go through. None of my close friends, nor anyone in my family, had survived a similar trauma. It felt like there was no one I could talk to about it who truly understood.

It took years to climb out of the depths of that loss to feel whole and happy again. I believed that my relationship with Kerry had been my only chance to receive unconditional love.

As I said, I was young, in love and naïve. I am so glad to have been wrong.

Years after Kerry died, I married Thom, a death and dying therapist. (Was that a coincidence?) We had many happy years together in the California desert. I had a stellar medical practice, an understanding husband, our two daughters, Caitlin and Justine, and every other weekend, my stepdaughter, Sarah. It was more love than I thought could exist.

Ten years after we married, we moved back to the town where I had grown up in Connecticut. Caitlin was eight years old, and Justine was three. Sarah was eighteen and going to college in Montana. Life had moved on.

The day we arrived in Connecticut was the same day my mother was diagnosed with colon cancer. In dealing with my mother's death three years later, Thom was a great help to me. Two years after that, he himself died of lung cancer. (I wrote about his last year in my book, *Living with a Dead Man*. No one I knew had as great a dying experience as Thom. No one. He used his knowledge to help us through one of the hardest years of my life. So I needed to tell his story.)

I call the grief that comes after a terminal illness "expected grief." Knowing the end is coming makes all the difference in the grieving process because you have the time to say your goodbyes and to address anything you need to resolve between you.

In relating these two different personal grieving experiences, I move back and forth in this book between Kerry's unexpected death, when I was young and my heart was shattered, and Thom's expected death, which broke my mended heart.

These stories are grouped loosely into five different parts dealing with the initial shock and surprise of their passings, handling things people say and do, trying to find a new "normal," experiencing firsts without these loved ones, and eventually moving on.

Eighteen years after Thom's death, I married Gene, who grew up in the town next to mine in Connecticut. He's a local guy I met four years after his wife died, but we have a lot more in common than being widow and widower.

We both feel we have been given another chance at one of the most important relationships in life. In letting go of what was, we have found what matters going forward. Allowing someone else into your heart is not easy, but it's so very worth the struggle. We are discovering that there are still many wonderful first experiences to be had in our senior years.

Just so you know, I am not still a mess. But I was—a couple of times. Those experiences made me who I am today. I did not plan to be a grief warrior. But that's who I am. At least, it's a big part of who I have become.

Because I am open about my history of loss, patients have shared their stories and feelings with me. They knew I would understand. Maybe I can help you with your grief by telling you my own stories and the insights I learned from them, as well as some of my patients' experiences, with names changed, of course.

It's not always easy to open up about feelings and experiences. No one enjoys being vulnerable, especially when it comes to the emotions they experience while grieving. But grief is something we all will live through at some point in our lives.

I hope by sharing these stories, you'll see that there's no one right answer to how you should grieve. They cover a range of experiences, some of which are difficult to believe and the raw emotion involved may not always be easy to understand. But if you are deeply mired in grief, I think you will relate to them.

Part 1. Shock and Surprise

The End Is the Beginning

*T*HE LOGICAL MIND tells us we are all going to die. Yet when someone does, our comfortable, secure, safe world may feel like a grenade was just tossed into it, whether or not that loss was expected. We stagger into the part of life that defies logic. The death itself is one thing. Life after that parting is a whole other thing. Death is an ending, and it marks when your life completely changed.

After the initial shock of your loved one's passing, you get busy with everything that then has to be done. (Even if you know that death is coming, it's still a shock when it does.) You contact family, friends, your employer, the funeral home, and your place of worship if you have one. Writing an obituary is no easy task either. Maybe you even need to locate a will.

All these tasks seem to be spelled out. Do this, do that. Decisions are made. This immediately-after-death business follows a course we each have to go through. You may have a lot of help from friends and family or none at all, but at some point, this busy phase ends and a new one begins. This starts the difficult stage of stitching your life together after your loss.

There are grief groups to attend (or not). There are mornings to get up (or not), food to eat (or not), friends to talk to (or not). Sometimes, knowing what to do can be overwhelming.

We are left to figure it out by ourselves. It's common to hide our pain and tears, put on a happy face, and do our grieving in solitude. We never see grief happening, even though it happens every day. We are all in it alone together.

Maureen is my best friend from high school. A few years after Thom's death, her daughter died. There was more than an hour-long wait in line at the wake before I reached the casket. After some time, I could see Maureen on the other end of the receiving line. She was going through the motions of shaking each person's hands as they cried and hugged her, then repeating the process with the next person. She was wrung out, almost transparent. Maureen's other daughter and her first husband (the father to her daughters) were beside her, and next to him was her second husband. Sadness and somberness clung to each of them like a smoky haze.

When I reached her, she looked surprised and then relieved. "Oh my God. *You* know what it's like! You get it."

As I held her in my arms, I whispered, "Yes, my love. I do get it. I understand where you are. You are doing a beautiful job. Hang in there. We will catch up later."

The receiving line at a wake is no place to have a detailed discussion. But people want to be able to offer support, however briefly, and to share your pain. And while it may not seem like enough, don't underestimate its significance.

At least the wake and funeral give people the chance to grieve together in the same space and time. For Maureen and me, understanding death's painful impact cemented our friendship further. And the fact that people showed up for the services meant so much to each of us.

For work colleagues or more distant friends, you will have at least looked each other in the eye once and acknowledged the loss together. It helps not to have to tell the story from the beginning each time you see someone. You steel your emotional self, get through it, then go home and pass out.

The truth is, no one tells you that despite feeling raw grief over your loss, at the wake and service, *you* are the one consoling everyone else. The weight of their grief is added to your own. I am not really sure how that happens, but it does.

When Kerry died, his wake was held in the bar he co-owned. When I finally worked up the courage to walk inside that night and saw everyone we knew there with sadness in their eyes, I became overwhelmed, burst into tears, and hid out in the ladies' room.

Not being able to face everyone at once, I refused to leave. I just could not do it. I was prepared to stay in there until everyone went home.

Vicky, a friend who worked as a nurse, suggested I see one person at a time. She kept guard at the bathroom door and, one by one, men and women came into the ladies' room to pay their respects. It was slightly less overwhelming, but doable.

It didn't even seem weird to me at the time! I got through it, but all I remember is being stuck in the ladies' room and Vicky being my rock. Now it seems bizarrely comical.

But if you are mourning someone you love, the venue really doesn't matter. You show up—even if it is in the ladies' room.

Wondering Why

*W*HY DID YOUR LOVED ONE DIE? Why did this have to happen? Why now? Why not later? Why did she die the way she did? Why did it have to be so quick? Or why did he have to suffer so long? Contemplating their death raises questions that beg to be answered:

- ∾ What was his life all about?
- ∾ Why couldn't we have more time?
- ∾ Why did she have to die?
- ∾ Why are we here?
- ∾ Why am I here?

There must be some reason things are the way they are. Death sets you on a quest to figure it all out.

We each find our own answers. Although I do not connect with organized religion, I do believe in a higher power. After forty-five years of working with and learning about the human body and all its beautiful, intricate workings, it is obvious to me that it is not simply the product of evolution. Add the mind and spirit to the body and you have a miraculous gift. (I feel the same awe for nature, the "world body" with all its animals, oceans and plants, and its equally, if not more, complex workings. And what about all the multifarious interactions between those worlds?)

If life is a gift, what am I supposed to do with mine? Is it a coincidence that I am here? When I look back on important events that shaped my life, I see patterns and connections. You might say these are coincidences, but I feel they are essential experiences. I would not be who I am or where I am without them. These are my personal answers, not only to how my life evolved, but to my own *whys*.

For example, I could have been on that plane with Kerry. In fact, we were up in the air minutes before, checking out the systems. When we were landing, my heart started racing and I felt short of breath. Kerry had to open the hatch so I could breathe fresh air. I almost felt pushed out of the plane.

Even now, I believe it was a sign that I was not supposed to be with Kerry when he crashed. I was supposed to live. I look back on that experience with awe and wonder.

Here is another example. I have four brothers, three older and one younger. The older ones often made my life challenging when we were young. A lot of times, they excluded me from their games and activities. Here is how it went: they would come up with a fun event for the day and ask my mom, "Can we go fishing (or swimming or skating) today?"

My mom's answer was usually, "Yes, but take Marianne with you."

They resented being the babysitters, so they took it out on me.

Not too long ago, our neighbor, a farmer, told me how the boys would head down to the fishing hole near his house. "There would be your brothers, all in a line with their fishing poles slung over their shoulders. Then there would be you, a hundred yards behind. They never let you walk with them." He shook his head like he was thinking "that's boys for you." That is just how it was. I still can't forget the time I was tied to the trunk of a big maple tree for an entire football game so they didn't have to watch me.

The point is that my brothers' harsh treatment of me just strengthened my inner self. I did not believe their baloney that I was not as good as they were because I was younger, smaller, a girl or anything else. Those trials opened my understanding of and empathy for others. They cemented in me a clear idea of what was right and what was wrong. For me, choosing to do the right thing was less a choice and more the obvious path to take. At least partially, I credit that belief to my experiences growing up.

The survival attitude instilled by my brothers allowed me to make it through a tough medical school and an even tougher internship and residency. As a smart, good-looking young woman, I encountered prejudices and verbal abuse regularly, easily far worse than my brothers' antics. But it was the survival skills my brothers honed in me that saved me—that and my stubbornness.

Looking back, I see hundreds of "coincidences" that have brought me to where I am today. Each trial was a gain. I know (often retrospectively) why things happened in my life. I know what I am here for and what I need to do to maximize the time

I have left. Am I clued in all the time? No. But I am trying to stay open.

Writing this book was prompted by one of those coincidences; just a simple request from a patient. "Dr. Bette, you have to write a book on grieving." That one sentence has changed my life significantly.

If we reflect on why things happened, we see the same principle is in play. The many times we could have (or maybe should have) had a severe or deadly accident, but didn't. The meeting we were not supposed to go to (and maybe did not want to go to), where we met a person who changed our lives.

These "coincidences" may suggest there is a design at work that we are not consciously aware of. It is subtle, but it is there. For me, there are no coincidences, only lessons. Now I look for the lessons and try to tap into them.

Sometimes I feel that in this lifetime, along with bountiful love, my lessons have to do with loss. How else could I understand the intense emotions of despair and sorrow or console my patients?

Experiencing those feelings has embedded in me a connection to grief so visceral that I don't even have to think about it. It is me in a way that defies description.

Sometimes friends would say, "You have such a positive attitude. How can you do that when you've had such loss in your life?"

That's when I tell them I have learned to appreciate my losses as gifts. They have opened my awareness in ways that nothing else could and connected me to understanding these lessons.

After Kerry died, my brother Pete shared an important idea that enabled me to stop beating myself up, looking for the answers not only for why Kerry had died but why I had not. He said, "By the time you get to a place where you can get answers to your questions, those answers won't matter anymore." That made sense to me then, and it still does.

Suicidal Thoughts

ANOTHER CAUSE of unexpected death is suicide, an ending where the person takes an active role. It could be an impulsive act or a planned one, or even an instance where a person simply puts themselves in risky situations that could easily lead to death.

Who would do such a thing? Why? Couldn't they be stopped? Why didn't they reach out to the people who loved them? And if friends and family knew their loved one's intention, wouldn't they intervene?

Before Kerry died, I never understood the workings of a suicidal mind. I had worked with families that were left wondering *why* after someone they loved had committed suicide. We were all shocked and confused together.

What I have come to realize is that the person thinking about suicide is not in their right mind. They are in a state of deep and tortured despair where the brain doesn't function normally. They are not unwilling, but unable, to see the truth that they will survive and love life again.

There are a series of immediate responses that happen to your body when you are under extreme stress. There are chemicals produced called "neurotransmitters" that affect brain functioning in an unusual way.

Several people have told me that their immediate reaction to shocking news of a loved one's death has been extremely physical. It is as if you have not only broken a bond with your lost loved one, but your normal neural pathways are suddenly broken also.

I believed Kerry was my one and only soul mate. With him gone, life would be a constant reminder of what I had lost and could never have again. Each day, I would have to live with a monstrous void. It would be more painful than I could bear.

When I heard the news of his crash, there was an immediate avalanche of uncontrolled feelings that overwhelmed my body. I couldn't breathe. I suffered from vomiting and diarrhea until I was empty. My mind, heart and body ran to different corners of the universe. Each part of me was screaming in pain. Pain, pain, pain. It felt like an explosion had gone off inside me and I was shattered into a million pieces, held together by a thin facade. I would never be whole again. So why bother?

Everyone I spoke to about Kerry's death was shocked and devastated. I could feel their pain too. Each minute, every hour. Pain, pain, pain. It escalated in a way that made it impossible to eat, sleep, walk, breathe or even see through my swollen eyes. There was no way to get away from the pain.

Most of all, I wanted to be with Kerry, wherever he was. I felt sure I could find him, even dead. Our connectedness would lead the way. It was the only thing that made me feel hopeful—being dead and finding Kerry. I could not live without him.

But my friends and family kept me alive, especially my sister Regina. She never left me alone, literally. Even when I went to the bathroom, she went with me, so I couldn't slit my wrists as I had planned.

My parents flew out from the East Coast and stayed two weeks. Regina and my best friends Sandy and Floyd, my stalwart bodyguards, moved in for a few days. I was in almost constant contact with at least one of those five people. They are the only reason I am alive and was not locked up in the psych ward at the hospital.

I don't remember much of those two weeks, but during that time, I let go of the idea of suicide. The change took hold when I had a conversation with Regina in my bathroom, during which she forced me to sit in hot water to calm the muscle spasms everywhere in my body. She sat on the side of the tub; me in, her out.

"You mean if I kill myself I won't be able to be with Kerry?" I asked.

"I don't think so," Regina replied.

"Why not?"

"Because people who kill themselves don't get to go to the same place as someone who just dies." Darn. That sounded like truth.

"So... I have to live through all this pain?" I asked, disbelieving.

"I think so."

"You are probably right. Shit."

"Right. We will be here for you."

"I don't think that will be enough."

After my second week under surveillance, my posse was reassured I would not kill myself. Two weeks were enough for me to figure out that one thing—no suicide. But I was not happy about it.

If I stayed alive, perhaps I could see Kerry again someday, somewhere, far into the future. There was not much else I could figure out. I was just barely insulated enough from the pain to understand that suicide was "the flawed logic of a person in deep despair tortured to the point of being unable to see the truth," as I once heard it described. In time, I hoped I would feel differently about living without Kerry.

Medical professionals know that if a person is a danger to themselves or others, they can legally be held against their will (usually sedated) for seventy-two hours in a psychiatric unit. Calling the police or ambulance often gets them there.

The benefit of that seventy-two-hour respite has been studied and proven, although I don't think anyone has figured out exactly how or why it happens. That time saves lives. It is magical. Your fractured mind starts to mend. In three days, you feel and think differently.

When it was time for my parents to leave two weeks after Kerry's death, I was terrified to be alone. I bawled like a baby when we said goodbye.

My dad, always the more emotional of my parents, held me tightly in his arms and petted my head. He whispered in my ear, "You have always been wanted and always been loved. Your mother had an operation to help her conceive again after your three brothers were born because she wasn't getting pregnant. We both wanted a curly-headed girl. We were so happy when you were born. You were so wanted and so loved. Remember that."

Surprisingly, I had never heard that story before. The timing could not have been more perfect. I was wanted and loved before I was here. I have remembered that conversation ever since.

The next day, my friends Sandy and Floyd were leaving too. They had both had abusive childhoods. With no family support, they had each pulled themselves together and made a good life on their own. Later, they found one another and married in middle age. But if anyone could understand how busted up I felt emotionally, it was them. If Sandy or Floyd said something was going to help me through, I believed it, and I did it. So I decided to seek their advice.

When it was time for everyone to go home to their respective lives, I cornered Sandy. "Sandy, what do I do when I'm all alone and don't know how to get from one minute to the next? How am I going to get by? Help!" I didn't say this to my parents since I felt they were weary enough.

"You hum," Sandy said.

"What?"

"You hum." She waited for it to register. It was like learning a foreign language.

"Like, what do I hum?" I asked disbelievingly.

"It doesn't matter what you hum," she replied. "It is *that* you hum. It could be just one note, the same note. Just hum. That will help to get you from one minute to the next." She said this in a way that told me she had done a lot of humming in her life.

Sometimes I hummed the most pathetic, high-pitched, shaky, single note that even I could not believe it came from me. But that one note, that one sound coming from deep inside my core, kept me grounded, connected to the here and now.

There were many lonely days filled with humming. What the heck? It was all I had. I was desperate.

Humming was with me wherever I went. Sometimes, I could do two things at the same time. I could think about humming, and I could hum. It helped. It really did.

If you are lost in the pain of grief, don't give up. I recommend giving humming a try. It's simple, and it is something that can keep you from coming unraveled.

And please know that it's not always going to be this hard. Living with a grieving heart does get easier. Those of us who have survived similar despair have discovered this by continuing to live.

Better yet, we've learned that love is not a onetime thing. It comes in many forms and will come again to you. Life is worth living, guaranteed.

Dad's Ashes

IF YOUR LOVED ONE IS CREMATED, after their death, you will receive a plastic box in the mail or an urn from the funeral home that weighs about ten pounds. It's astonishing how heavy those ashes are. Despite going through this a few times, I am still surprised when they show up.

When they arrive, you have to decide what to do with them. There are some laws about what can and cannot be done, depending on where you live.

With my husband's ashes, the girls and I divided them among the four of us. Justine took her share into the woods, where she often played. Caitlin went down to the river for her own personal closure ceremony. Sarah went to the Pacific with hers. I placed most of mine on each side of our driveway, as a protective guard to our property, and the rest in our favorite flower garden with Mom's ashes.

Saying what we did with his ashes is easy, but doing it took a little special energy. It happened years after he died, when we were all home together on Thom's birthday. The truth is, I was tired of having them in the back of the closet. It was way past time to get them out of the house.

My dad's ashes were sent to my younger brother, Pete. Our father's request was to have some of his ashes spread in the ocean, since he was a Seabee in the United States Navy in World War II. Pete also insisted that each of Dad's six children have a share of the ashes. Not sure why, but he was insistent, and no one fought the idea.

My share went in the flower garden, next to Mom's and Thom's ashes. I am not sure what everyone else did with their shares, but one of my brothers—the one just older than me, Jim—was slightly estranged from the rest of us and lived in Georgia. Since ashes aren't the kind of thing we wanted to just send him in the mail, Pete and I concocted a plan for me to travel to Georgia while I was on a trip to Asheville to see my daughters.

It was the perfect excuse to do some sorely needed reconnecting with Jim. At first, it was a little awkward being together again—partly because this was a new and different place and partly because of the reason we were together, namely to pass along Dad's ashes. But darn, I was glad to see him. We were able to spend an enjoyable few hours together and did indeed reconnect.

Who knew the power of ashes? Our father had brought us together again. Thanks, Dad.

There is no set time or rule to tell a person when to dispose of ashes and let intense grieving come to an end. Somehow, sometime, you feel ready and then you follow through. You let go. It can be freeing.

Several patients of mine have their loved one's ashes in urns in their homes. This of course makes them more portable. One of my patients, an eighty-three-year-old lady whom I will call "Vivian," takes her husband's ashes from the mantle to the kitchen table each day and talks to him over breakfast. The ashes go back on the mantel for the day, but are then again moved to the bedroom at night.

We had many conversations about her husband's expected death while he was in hospice, but this was one of the earliest conversations after his death. "Dr. Bette, do you think it's okay if I take his urn with me and talk to him?"

"It's not that uncommon," I said. "Often, a person will feel comforted by having the ashes nearby, like you do with your husband's. If it helps you feel good, I see no reason not to."

A look of relief swept across Vivian's face and her shoulders seemed to relax a bit. Maybe she needed that permission from her family doctor, telling her she was okay.

"Oh, I know he's dead," she said. "I am not denying that. But somehow it keeps our connection going." What could possibly be wrong with that? And the number of people who do similar things might surprise you.

Another patient of mine, whom I'll call Rebecca, took this to an extreme. She was in her fifties when her older sister died, and she kept her sister's ashes in a brass urn. She took them with her everywhere she went, apart from work. If she went to the store, she had her sister's ashes seat-belted in the passenger seat of the car. She took them across the street, from her house to the barn, twice a day when she cared for her horses. Then they were in the kitchen when she made dinner and in the bedroom at night.

Unlike Vivian, Rebecca did this for years. Each time she came for a doctor's visit, I would inquire about the status of her sister's ashes.

"Oh, fine," she would answer flatly. "I still take her everywhere with me." No, she didn't want to talk to a counselor about it.

I was concerned that this behavior was abnormal grieving, primarily due to the length of time it went on. She obviously wasn't concerned and continued to work and manage her everyday life. I left the lines of communication open, so if she started to unravel, I could steer her to a place where she could get help.

I did not see her for a few years, but when she was ready to retire from her job, she came in for an "exit" visit. She had decided to move to South Carolina, and she was taking her sister's ashes with her.

We talked about finding her sister a final resting place. She spoke about the land she had bought, and by the end of her visit, she thought she would finally bury her sister's ashes on a south-facing knoll where the sun shone all day. When she moved, she felt her life would change for the better, and she would finally be able to let her sister go.

Rebecca's grief taught me that denial can at times be your friend. It allows your brain to process your trauma at a later time, when you can handle it and still function at the same time. Grief can wait for you.

Stages of Grief

*G*OD BLESS ELIZABETH KÜBLER-ROSS. She was a psychia-
trist practicing in the 1960s who took care of dying patients.
Through her patients' stories, she taught medical doctors about
a very important part of life: dying.

Before then, physicians often felt that if their patient was
dying, they had somehow failed. Often, patients were left to
face the end of their life without the emotional support of
their own doctor.

The insights Kübler-Ross wrote about in her book
On Death and Dying in 1969 arose from interviews between
her and her dying patients: a discussion about their life ending.
These insights enlightened the medical community to focus
on emotional empathy and understanding. She also taught
that death is an opportunity for those involved to have a spiritual awakening.

Medical doctors usually follow an outline or set of procedural rules that lead to successful results when diagnosing or treating an illness. Kübler-Ross filled in that missing outline for death: the stages of grief.

But she would turn over in her grave, as my Irish mother would have said, in shock and disappointment at how those stages are now being used; not so much by physicians, but by the public.

When a person dies, friends don't know how to be supportive to the griever. So they google "grief" and eventually find Kübler-Ross's "The Stages of Grief." Now they think they have a roadmap. "Gee," they wonder, "where is my friend in these stages?" In our fast-paced world, we want answers, we want them now, and the internet reinforces the belief that quick answers are always a click away.

People, however, do *not* follow stages as they grieve and while they may experience all of them at different times, they will experience them in a random order and revisit ones they thought they'd already gotten through. For anyone to think that there is some prescribed outline a person should follow while grieving is rather ridiculous. Kübler-Ross's work was done with dying patients, and it does not always apply to the rest of us, those of us who are left behind.

Neither should we be looking at the stages as an emotional prescription for grief. They will be some help, but one of the worst things you can do to someone who is grieving is to try to identify what stage of mourning they are in. This treats grief as a cold scientific fact rather than the intensely personal feeling that it is. It also falsely leads you to believe that one stage leads to the next, and that after completing all the stages, you graduate and, voilà, the grief is over.

But there is no finish line with grief. It never happens like that. Really. *Never.* Identifying your current stage of grief can make you feel like you are being graded. That can leave you feeling misunderstood and isolated, especially when someone else tries to apply that label for you. It can be one of the most hurtful things people do.

This is exactly the opposite of Kübler-Ross's intentions. She planned to teach us how to have a conversation between two people, the dying patient and the doctor. There is no instruction book for dying or grief, and it is probably best that there is not. It could rob us of the need and experience that we may only get once in our lifetime. Grieving is uniquely personal. It is an opportunity to make a significant spiritual connection for ourselves.

That is why I haven't listed the stages of grief here. They are labels to help health professionals become aware of the insights and opportunities that can only happen at life's end. Even then, they are so often misunderstood. Not everyone goes through the stages of life in the same way (like puberty and menopause), and so it is with dying, death and grieving. Everyone ends but not on the same page.

Instead, I would recommend reading Kübler-Ross's quotes. Those are awesome, and they will teach you everything you need to know from her. And yes, you can find them on the internet.

Dealing with Anger

*A*NGER IS A PART OF GRIEF. It just is. And it's for darn sure not rational. It is 100 percent emotional. Anger comes after the shock of a death or a terminal diagnosis. It has an energy all its own. Anger can move you in ways that loss, depression and perhaps love never could. It is powerful and often comes out in a negative way.

I needed to fight to keep control of my anger. There was never any chance of me burying it. It always felt like a rattle-snake curled up in my core, shaking its rattles like it wanted to strike. But it would not control my actions.

I struggled to release my anger in ways that wouldn't destroy me or those around me. Sometimes, I would scream, swear, run, throw rocks or cry until there were no more tears or snot left in my body. I would physically exhaust myself so…

I could *feel* something besides rage.

I could *take* a full breath.

I would *be able* to survive.

I would *accept* what had happened to me.

I could *believe* that it was supposed to be this way.

I could *live* with the unanswered questions.

I could *believe* I would be whole again—scarred, but whole.

I could *believe* that someday I would see beauty.

I would *feel* like laughing and maybe even fall in love again.

I would *not* let anger control my mind, leaving me unable to hope for a full, productive, happy life.

I would *not*. I would find a way. Anger would have to be tamed, and I would have to do the hard work of taming it. No one else could do it for me.

The anger I felt after Thom died was much milder than the anger after Kerry's passing. The difference was that Kerry was young, his death was accidental and immediate, and we were madly in love. We hadn't been together long enough for our lives together to become more settled. Our love was all still fresh and exciting and new. Thom and I had been married for fifteen years, and we'd had time together to grow accustomed to the idea of his passing.

Before Kerry, my only experience with death had been the passing of my grandparents and hospitalized patients I had treated. Even being a doctor and having dealt with several deaths had not prepared me for what I had to cope with.

Helping someone else deal with a death was nothing like experiencing a loss myself. Maybe Kerry's death somehow prepared me for Thom's. Knowing Thom had cancer and seeing it fail to respond to all the chemo and radiation was a dose of reality: he was going to die. That year of chemo and radiation gave me time to prepare for his death. I was still angry, but it was nothing like my full-blown rage after Kerry. (Thank God!)

One of my patients, who I'll call Alice, had a completely different experience with anger. First, her anger never fully blossomed until after her husband's death, in large part because, at the end of his life, he had dementia. There were many things he said or did that were extremely hurtful, not only while he had dementia, when he was even worse, but also before. There were times he mistreated her or her family, which she later realized came from his jealousy.

Alice and her siblings shared a lot of unconditional love, and he was jealous of that. If she perceived a need in a loved one, she could usually find a way to fulfill that need. I guess when her husband—who was obviously attracted to and a recipient of that love—compared himself and his abilities to Alice, he could never measure up. Too bad he felt he had to.

But the anger she rightly felt took years after his death to dissipate. This was not because she didn't feel it anymore, but because, once she realized he had dementia, there was no way for him to help heal the wounds he had inflicted. She had to stuff her anger away.

Alice also felt restrained from showing her anger because she thought it would be perceived as inappropriate. Emotions connected with death, especially anger, are not considered publicly acceptable.

There is just so much we have to figure out in the privacy of our own hearts. Opening up to these emotions is an unburdening that heals. She and I bonded over our "widowness."

She was like I had been when Kerry died—inexperienced and often unsupported because, to the untrained eye, she looked like she was doing okay. No one she knew had had this experience yet. She was a groundbreaker.

Alice and I have had many conversations about our independently shared experience. Over and over in my work, I have seen the consequences of deep, unreleased resentments to the physical body. If you are at a loss for someone with whom it is safe to share these feelings, ask around for a good grief therapist. You might be surprised by how many people have one. They are experts in this area, and you can find them everywhere.

Alice took years to be ready to let that anger go, but she did it—or more correctly, is still doing it.

Shoulda, Coulda, Woulda, If Only…

*W*HEN THOM RECEIVED HIS CANCER DIAGNOSIS, I was struggling with how this could have happened. I flashed back to a thought I'd had a few months earlier that he should talk to his doctor about getting a lung cancer screening. He had been a smoker for years before I knew him. In recent years, he had mostly stopped, and then mostly sneaked. But he had no symptoms, so the screening never happened.

When he was diagnosed with lung cancer later that year, I beat myself up with the idea that I *should* have got him to get his screening done—it *could* have saved his life. *Would* that have made any difference? Let me tell you, though, it took a long time to accept that I couldn't have changed his fate.

Ten years after Thom died, the medical protocol of screening heavy smokers for lung cancer came about thanks to a new technology: a spiral CT scan of the chest. It knocked the breath right out of me.

"Oh my goodness, *if only* he *could* have waited to develop cancer, we *would* have found it and saved him. He *could* be alive today!"

That same feeling hit me years later, when a new chemotherapy was developed for lung cancer that had really great results.

These emotions sprung from my heart. It's funny how the bargaining, the feeling that we could control someone else's life, keeps coming back. It is still part of the grieving process, and therefore part of healing. Everyone has these thoughts.

But the truth is, you have no control over someone else's life. Their destiny is their own. The lessons and meaning of their life are theirs alone. You can be a witness to their life and their choices, but you cannot change what they need to learn or how they learn it.

There is another important type of "should" that people have often shared with me after their loved one's death. "I should have treated them better."

The powerful role a loved one plays in our life is often not apparent until they die. That empty space in your life that they left behind is now so obvious. How could you have missed it? Why didn't you know? Why didn't you appreciate her more? Why didn't you tell him how important he was when he was alive?

So often, we have not learned how to share our most powerful emotions: love and anger. We can be stingy about speaking tender words. Often anger is easier to access and express than love and tenderness.

The awareness that comes after a death is a gift. If you have felt sadness or guilt about what you wished you had said, but didn't, you will have to ask for forgiveness from the person you lost, and also from yourself. You didn't know then what you know now. Let me repeat that for you. You didn't know then what you know now.

You cannot go back and change the past. They knew how it was between you, the importance of what you had. They knew the love that was there and that you did your best under the circumstances. Try to let it go.

But now that you are better aware of the importance of emotional language, shower those you know with love. If you are still unsure how to express it, get a card or poem or song that does so for you and give it to them. Tell them you are new at this "love expression business," and this is your first effort.

There is real power and beauty in any act of love.

Decisions, Decisions, Decisions

RIGHT AFTER KERRY DIED, my friend Vicky (who was also Kerry's best friend) suggested we move to Alaska. The plan was to leave the pain and suffering behind and start out fresh in a new place with no reminders of what had been. She thought it was a great idea.

I considered it, but I couldn't do it. I am a stubborn person. The idea that there might be a place on this Earth where I couldn't go because it was too painful just didn't feel right. Besides, where would I go to get away from all the mental anguish? Wherever I went, I would have to take my beat-up heart and head with me. I knew there was no place out there where I would feel better. No place better than where I was.

So, I committed to staying put and working through my loss, even though I had no idea how that might happen. When the time did come for me to move, I hoped to have recovered significantly from my grief so I could leave with less emotional baggage.

When a spouse or partner dies, everyone has an opinion about whether the one left behind should move or stay put. What I have often seen happen after an older person loses their spouse is that the children decide that the surviving parent has to move, dump the clothes, sell the car, and get rid of the dog. How the heck the surviving spouse gets through all that is beyond me.

I understand how the grieving brain works—or more correctly, how it does not work. Adding the trauma of all those additional changes is another loss. I encourage any grieving person to sit tight, if at all possible, until they feel like moving. The grieving person's opinion should trump all others.

I stayed in the desert in the same house for eighteen wonderful years. Well… okay, the first three were pretty tough, but it was great after that. I married Thom, had my girls, and had the medical practice of my dreams. In short, I stayed and made my dreams come true. Thom died three years after we moved to Connecticut, and I still live in the house we built.

Staying put worked well for me both times. I think I might have seriously unraveled on each occasion if I'd had to pack up and move out. Where would I have gone? What would I have taken? What would I have left behind? Initially, the comfort of the house was important, but in each house, I made additions and renovations that gave the home new life.

Gene and I have made significant changes to our house. Some things look the same, but even those feel brand new because our home contains our combined energy. Now that I'm retired, I have honestly never enjoyed this house and its surroundings more. It is a sheer pleasure to be here.

About a year after Thom died, I took everything out of his closet and laid it all on our king-sized bed, where the girls and I went through it. What we didn't want would go to the thrift shop supporting the battered women's shelter. Thom's signature Hawaiian silk shirts were pretty well shared between Caitlin and Justine.

I went about the busy work of packing up dress shirts, slacks and shorts in big black plastic bags. Justine and Caitlin each had armloads of the clothes they wanted to keep.

I missed what Justine was up to. Suddenly, I heard her talking, but her voice was muffled and she sounded far away. That was when I saw movement under a pile of Thom's clothes.

"Oh, Mom," she said as she took in a few deep breaths. "These smell just like Dad."

I had not expected that. Her ability to still smell her father shocked me. In fact, I didn't know it was even possible for his scent to still be there after a year.

Once, one of my patients had asked about how the girls were doing. I related that story, and she just nodded her head slowly and said, "Yeah, I know. The scent is usually gone after about three years." That also surprised me, both that she knew and that it took three years.

To this day, I have Thom's fancy cowboy boots sitting on the top shelf of my closet. They are there not in remembrance of Thom, but because I love those boots and if I wear a pair of heavy socks, they fit me. Occasionally I wear them with a long skirt—my dressy cowgirl outfit—and they look great on me.

My advice is to keep anything that gives you pleasure. At some point, you will let it all go. You'll know when the time is right.

Asking for Help

*A*BOUT FIVE MONTHS after Thom died, the mortgage rates dropped. It was over a 2 percent decrease, and my banker told me, "You should remortgage." Lowering my monthly payment was just what I needed now that I was a widow and a single mom. He gave me the paperwork.

At home, I took our old mortgage documents from the file cabinet and set them on the small kitchen desk. Not only had the forms changed, but since I was now single and widowed, I had to include a copy of Thom's death certificate. I was coasting along the bumpy road of paperwork until I took out the death certificate and held it in my hand. There, along with his name, age, address and birthday, was his cause of death (metastatic lung cancer) and the contributing cause (smoking).

In one breath and three heartbeats, I went through shock, anger, bargaining, acceptance and depression—turmoil that ganged up on me when I least expected it. My eyes filled up, and the paperwork got stuffed back into a drawer. If I had been lifting fifty-pound weights, I could not have felt more spent.

Each week, when I went to the bank, I promised to get the papers back to my banker. Each week, I lied.

One day at lunch, I ran over to the mini-mall across the street from work. I was coming out of a phone store when a big, new, gray, four-door pickup truck pulled up to the sidewalk next to me and the passenger window slid down. It was the banker behind the wheel. He waved.

"Hi, Tony."

"Hi, Dr. Bette. I am wondering when you are going to get that paperwork back to me."

Walking to the open window, I felt my nostrils flare and the tops of my ears prickle. Over time and after too many experiences to count, I had come to recognize this as my first sign of anger. My inner voice was now reacting pretty quickly. It said, "Stay cool." How was I to tell this guy I was incapacitated by the task? I leaned into the cab.

"Tony," I said, "remember in the old days in Italy, a widow would wear black for a year after her husband died?"

He nodded his head.

"I think it was to remind everyone in the town that she was in mourning and that she needed help."

"Yeah," he croaked.

"Well, nowadays, we don't wear black like that. We look okay, but we are not any better than in the old days. Grief is like carrying a big wet blanket draped over you. You can see the ground in front of you. You can even lift it up to look ahead, though it takes a lot of effort. But the thing is, you cannot put the blanket down. No one sees it but you. You look normal, but you are not. You are dragging the heavy, invisible, blanket weight of a life gone off the track."

I could see the empathy in his eyes as he digested this information.

"Honestly, I can't do it. I want to do it, but every time I hold that death certificate, I... I just can't do anything else." My voice cracked. "I honestly don't know when I will be able to do it." I motioned with a tilt of my head, my eyebrows inched up, hunching my shoulders and turning my palms face-up to show how lost I was.

He got it. He was Italian.

"Well," he said, "I could help you."

"I don't want to come to the bank and start crying in front of everyone," I said.

"No problem. I'll come to your office, and we can fill the forms out together in private. We'll get it done."

I didn't even know that could happen. I felt like I had just won the lottery. Somehow, asking for help did not even occur to me. Why didn't it? It still surprises me that asking for help was not in my vocabulary, for whatever reason. I vowed to extinguish that habit right then and there. People love to help, they really do.

Here is what you say. "I need help." Or you can ask, "Can you help me?"

As soon as you say either of those things, it is like waving a red flag. People stop what they were doing or thinking and become clued into you. Now you have their complete attention and desire to help.

Even if you don't know what you need, you now have a partner in figuring it out. You could be in a crisis, but your listener is not. They may have some sage advice you wouldn't have been able to figure out for yourself. Simply ask for help.

Part II. Things People Say and Do

Hurtful Things People Say

*M*Y OLDER BROTHERS had more influence on my reactions in life than I previously knew. Being a tomboy growing up, I joined right in with their physical antics as a way of settling disagreements. This ranged from tickling to pushing and shoving to outright fistfights. If I sat back and acted "like a girl," they would have decimated me. So I learned at an early age to be pretty good at defending myself, which was a hard habit to break.

There was an Ear, Nose and Throat (ENT) doctor who, weeks after Kerry died, caught me in the hallway of the hospital while I was working in the emergency room. I don't recall what she said initially, but I do remember these words. "You are young and beautiful. You will get over it and find someone else."

My body temperature rose a few degrees after that last sentence. Immediately, I was flooded with sweat. My ears felt hot, and my breathing sputtered. I had to lock my knees to keep from collapsing. Cemented to the spot, I fixated on her nose. My hands were clenched, as if they had a mind of their own. I kept blinking while staring at her nose and thinking how funny it would be for me to break the nose of an ENT.

She was still talking. I heard nothing until she said, "Next time, make sure you pick a specialist." (Kerry was neither an MD nor a specialist.) She said it like my mother would say, "Next time at the supermarket, pick better-looking tomatoes than the ones you got last time." I didn't hear anything else after that.

Instead, this was the dialogue going on in my head.

THE ANGRY ME: Go ahead, punch her in the nose. She deserves it. (*She had denied my pain, planned my future, and insulted Kerry, all in two sentences.*)

THE NICE ME: You can't do that.

THE ANGRY ME: Yeah, I can. I'd like to see her nose broken and bent to the left. Maybe then she would know how pain feels. (*The cold-hearted bitch!*)

THE NICE ME: If you do that here, in the hospital's hallway, everyone will know.

THE ANGRY ME: So what? (*Maybe I could do it some-where else?*)

THE NICE ME: So... What everyone will remember is that you decked the ENT doc and broke her nose. It doesn't matter that she deserved it.

THE ANGRY ME: So what? Nobody likes her anyway.
(*I envisioned her lying on the hospital floor, screaming and writhing as bright red blood poured out of her nose into her cupped hands.*)

THE NICE ME: It will ruin your reputation. And you are just building a great one here.

THE ANGRY ME: Okay. (*My bloody mental pictures evaporated.*) Damn. It would have almost been worth it.

It took every drop of willpower I had to turn away from her and just walk off. I never said a word.

If this ever happens to you, *run* before you do something you will regret. No idiot is worth sacrificing your career or winding up in jail for.

More than anything, at that moment, my anger wanted the satisfaction of decking her. I am glad I didn't. But still…

When Communication Fails

*S*EVERAL MONTHS AFTER KERRY DIED, one of my acquaintances called to see how I was doing. I said I was okay. I lied. I was clearly not okay. But then, how do you jump into the whole mess when someone calls? At some point, she asked if I had some "peace and understanding" as to Kerry's meaning in my life. What had she been reading?

This was someone with no understanding of death, trying to tie up my feelings, nice and tidy. Then she could feel as though I had skipped to acceptance with a meaningful insight, just so she could feel better. Maybe she had reached that point in relation to his death, but I absolutely had not.

"Look, I can't talk to you about this now. Maybe in a few years I will be able to, but not now. I know you are trying to help, but I don't see any 'peace or understanding' on the horizon. I'm not even sure there *is* a horizon. I only see a big black hole where my life used to be." I hung up. I was going to sit there with my sad feelings, not forever, but just for now, while I sorted myself out.

The truth is that no one can really understand someone else's pain unless they have been through a similar loss—and even then, it's only a similar understanding. Everyone's loss is different. Even if you and your best friend both lost your spouses, your relationships were not identical, so how could your losses, your grief, your lives alone be the same?

It could have been worse. She could have said, "I know how you feel."

No one knows how you feel. Sometimes *you* don't even know how you feel. Grief is all-consuming and overwhelming. If someone had said they knew how I felt, it would have really set me off—not cause for a bloody nose, but God only knows what I would have said.

What I know now is what she really meant: I know you are hurting, and I want the pain to stop because I care about how you feel.

Communication of intense feelings is not easy. We don't have the practice or maybe even the vocabulary. Be gentle, not only with yourself, but also with your friends and family. They're trying to reach out to you, no matter how they say it.

When Someone Wants to Help

*P*EOPLE OFTEN ASK a grieving person, "What can I do for you?" After both Kerry and Thom's deaths, my usual response to that question was, "I have no (freaking) idea." What I felt like pointing out was, "I am in a fog right now, and you are asking me to put my grief aside, search around in the aftermath of my life, and come up with an idea of something you can do for me." Weird, but people do it all the time.

One of my grammar school friends, John, called three weeks after Thom died. "You haven't called me up!" he said, as if I had disappointed him. "I know you need help with those girls. I can help you. I can take them to and from school, or to the dentist. I can drive Justine to and from the horse barn. Use me."

Surprisingly, not only did I take him up on it, but he and Justine bonded over those trips to the barn. It's twenty years later, and whenever we talk, he always asks about Justine (and her horse).

My cousin Bob had his own brush with cancer and death, so he knew I could use help. He called me a couple of months later. After the small talk, he said, "I am coming down Saturday morning from Boston. I will be there by eight. I am going to work for you all day. You will make lunch for us both. And I will leave in the afternoon to be back home in time for dinner."

"Bob, what are you going to do here? What work?" I was utterly confused.

"Make a list," he said, like it was obvious.

"What are you talking about, Bob? I don't have anything to put on a list," I whined.

"You will. You have a week to make a list. I will see you Saturday morning."

"Okay, Bob, but I don't know." At that moment, telling me to make a list seemed like asking me to keep the *Titanic* from sinking.

"That's okay," he said happily, "you will." And he hung up.

When I realized he wasn't joking, I remembered that Bob and I had always had a lot of laughs together, so maybe that would be all we needed to do that day.

All week, though, I thought of things that could go on the list. All the things that had broken, were left undone, or should have been done after Thom's death. I had let so many things go.

By the time Bob arrived, I had a list, and so did Bob. "Have you changed the air filters lately?" One glance at my dumbfounded face told him the answer to that. "Okay, let's do that. How about the gutters? Don't answer, I saw the crap sticking out of the top of them. If you let them fill up and freeze, the ice will pull them right off the house."

I had no idea about air filters, and gutters were the last thing on my mind. We combined and prioritized our lists, and the day flew by. The love and support that came out of that man was beyond description, and the bonus was that I didn't have to think or talk about Thom's cancer the whole time. I will never forget that day, and we had a few good laughs as well—soul food.

My point is Bob used his talent and common sense to figure out what I needed. Anyone can do the same—a seasonal chore that must be done; washing the car or, better yet, detailing it; taking the kids or a dog for a walk; weeding the garden; taking you out for a scenic ride or maybe pizza and a movie. The list goes on and on once you get rolling.

The most common thing people do is to bring food. If someone can coordinate which foods are brought and when, that in itself can be helpful and save needless trips to the food bank with piles of dishes that arrived all at the same time.

You could also make a list of things friends can pick up for you. If anything comes to mind, write it down. The list could include things like making a meal, cleaning the house, doing the laundry, driving the kids, shopping, house maintenance, car maintenance, or anything else that comes to mind. Anything. Then, when someone asks what they can do, pull out the list and give them some choices. There are some great online resources to help coordinate help, like mealtrain.com and carecalendar.com.

People really want to help you. They may have no idea how to do that, but the desire to reach out to you is very real. Having a list is a great way for two people to communicate a need and the desire to help.

Be gentle. Be patient. And most of all, *breathe.*

How to Handle Others' Grief

ONE OF THE CHALLENGES you may encounter is how to handle the grief that other people are feeling. For example, someone telling you how badly they feel for you—it's fine at the wake and funeral, when we are all in a mess together, but after that it is not okay.

You may be having a fairly decent day—no dissolving into a puddle. Then when you are shopping at the grocery store, someone comes up all teary-eyed, grabs your hand, and says how awful they feel about your loss. Well, not only does that make you feel the wave of grief, but it also imposes guilt about having had a few decent minutes while in the produce department.

Sometimes, people ask, "How is your day going?" or "How are you doing?" Then, you get to set the tone of the conversation. If you were in survival mode, you could say so; or if you were actually having a decent day, you could say that.

It sounds simple, and it *is* simple—but it is also profound. When two people talk, a connection is made. That connection has meaning. It holds a healing magic. It says the most important nonverbal things. It says, you're cared about. They care about what you are going through in your life. They may not understand it, but they want to bear witness to it. They want to be on the other end of a connection with you.

If you have a friend at work, ask them to run interference for you by asking coworkers to hold off on approaching you about your grief until you feel ready. At work, Wendy and I came up with a plan to keep me from bawling on and off all day. As she ushered each person into the exam room, she would tell them, "Do not ask Dr. Bette how she is doing. Please just stick to the reason for the visit. It will really help her." I could see the caring in my patients' eyes and also the desire to ask how I was, but they were willing to hold back their questions as requested. This allowed me to stay in "doctor mode" and not fall back into what was going on in my personal life.

Initially, Wendy also did not ask how I was. After all our years working together, the family deaths we each went through, both in her family and mine, as well as the deaths of our patients, one look told volumes.

At the end of the day, one of us would say, "You did really well today." That meant the tissue quotient was low. Then we would just look at each other, understanding that tomorrow would be easier. Or maybe we would end the day in a well-needed hug. That was how we helped each other climb out of the mire of our grief at work.

If either of us was having a bad day, we would say to the other, "Double-check me. I am having a rough day."

For sure, some days were worse than others. But we almost never both had the same bad day.

What Other People Say

AFTER THOM DIED, not only did I feel protective of my children's mental health, but I was also totally responsible for their wellbeing, as only a single parent can be. I connected with their teachers and kept Caitlin in touch with her friends and Justine with the horses. However, you never know what other people might say to your kids.

One day, as I drove Justine to the horse barn, it was quiet in the car in that heavy sort of way. Something was going on with my daughter. So, I did the hardest thing—I stopped talking and waited for her to say something.

"Mom, I'm sorry I haven't been strong for you," she croaked.

"What are you talking about, Justine?"

"The secretary at school told me I have to 'be strong for you,' because Dad died and you would be feeling so bad. So, I was supposed to be strong for you and not cry." Now she was sobbing, her body coughing and sputtering as she tried not to cry. I pulled the car off the road.

"Justine, we have to talk about this." I waited for her to look at me, then I looked directly into her as only a mom can do. "That is not true. It is so not true. She was wrong to say that at all, but she was especially wrong to say that to you."

I could see that the reality was sinking in for her—an adult had told her a lie. I was furious. What had this woman been thinking? Asking an eight-year-old child to be strong for her mom! Here I felt *I* had all the responsibility for our mental health, and yet my child believed she was a failure at being emotionally responsible for me. No child should be told those words or feel compelled to heed them.

"In general, honey, we need to listen to what adults say at school, but in this case, you need to know that woman was totally out of line. Actually, change that to just plain wrong. Justine… Look at me, honey." She faced me, and I saw the rivulets of tears running down both cheeks. "If an adult, or anyone, tells you something that doesn't feel right, I want you to question it and ask me about it."

Now her shoulders relaxed, and tension released its hold. It was like the feeling in the air after a storm has passed, clean and calm.

"We are on the same team, you and me. We can talk about all the hard things, right?"

She nodded her head.

At this point, I was trying to stem my murderous thoughts about the school secretary and focus on relieving my child from a crippling responsibility.

"Promise me you will let me know if anyone else says odd things to you. Okay?"

She nodded again.

We held hands and sat for a few minutes while I checked my anger and shared the tissues.

When we arrived at the horse barn, I could have gone on and on about that witch, but I saw Justine looking at the horses. She was gazing at the painted pony, and it was staring back at her. Disconnected from grief, she was connecting with the horses.

Justine's bond with her horse taught me the amazing spirituality of such a powerful animal. It was as if her horse knew Justine's burdens and was absorbing whatever suffering it could from her.

She hopped out of the car with a lightness that told me she was my carefree child again, safe as she can be without a dad, no longer carrying the burden of worrying about the impact of his loss on me, her surviving parent.

"Thanks, Mom."

She turned back to me before closing the car door, pointed to her eye, made a heart shape with her hands, then pointed back at me. A nonverbal "I love you."

I blew her a kiss, and she scurried to her horse.

Hanging onto the steering wheel with both hands, as if it could give me strength, I rested my forehead between them and prayed, "Help me be a better parent. Remind me to be grateful for the chance to be one." I wished that Thom and my mom were there to help me.

You can't know what people will tell your child, or how your child will interpret what they see or hear. So it's important to ask questions like, "What are your friends saying to you?" or "Do you have anything you'd like to ask about so-and-so's death?" This provides a starting point for understanding what your child is thinking and feeling, and a chance to vali-date them.

Seeing adults crying, hugging and sharing feelings lets children know that grieving is an important part of life. Your child will take their cues from you. Being part of a community that sticks together teaches them not only the importance of sharing feelings but that love heals and they will be okay.

Part III. Trying to Be Normal

Going Crazy and Coming Back

SOMEONE GAVE ME AN IMAGE that I have since held as my own belief. We each live in a large sphere that defines our reality. We travel around inside our big reality bubble, but when someone close to us dies, that death tears a hole in it. As we start to heal, there are parts of our world that feel unaffected, but then we hit the hole where that loved one was and are forced out of our reality.

Once you exit that hole, there are no handholds or markers of where you are or should be. It's a place where time and the dimensions of our everyday world do not exist.

It can be scary out there. Kerry's death was the first experience that ripped a huge hole in my reality sphere. Initially, I was out of my world as much as I was in it.

Several weeks after he died, it was time to do the things I had previously thought of as normal. Returning to work in the emergency room, I was worried grief had fried parts of my medical knowledge. My nurse friends assured me that my brain would work just fine. They would watch me and let me know if I was going off the mark.

My friends were right. Work was a refuge of normality for my grieving brain. It was a great surprise and relief as my job became a respite for me.

At home, I had my dogs, who were also a refuge. One of them was named Magic. He was a one-hundred-pound, black-and-white malamute I inherited from Kerry. However, Magic was totally untrained when I got him.

One day, I tripped while walking him and he pulled me about fifty feet before I could stop him. Sled dogs are taught to pull, so I am sure he thought that was what he was supposed to do despite my screaming at him to stop.

Either Magic had to obey me or I would have to give him away, which I did not want to do. Vicky, my nurse-friend and dog connection, recommended taking obedience classes with Magic to see if that might help. Each day, Magic and I would go for long walks, then I worked with him for twenty minutes on each prescribed command and played with him after, as the instructor suggested.

We had a new lesson each of the ten weeks: sit, stay, come, down, heel and more. Each week, we grew closer. He knew what he was supposed to do and enjoyed making me happy. At the end of the course, he could have been the poster dog for obedience. It was more rewarding than I could have hoped for. That bond was magical.

People would ask me what I did the rest of the week. I was dumbfounded when I had no answer. "I have no idea!" It struck me as odd that there even was a "rest of the week."

A life revolving around work, weekdays and weekends didn't exist for me. It was just work and then time with the dogs.

Looking back, I can make some guesses about why my sister Regina and my friends started coming over and staying a lot more often. Or maybe my staring out into space gave my fried brain time to heal. Who knows? Perhaps that is a grieving brain just trying to heal and not feel plain ol' crazy anymore.

Sometimes, I just could not think or feel. My emotional self was exhausted. Sitting on the couch looking out over the Antelope Valley from my mountaintop home, I felt tethered, like a balloon on a very long string, hundreds of feet in the air. I was outside the hole in my reality.

You know that vision of the astronaut who space walks outside of the shuttle with lifelines connecting her to the inside? That was me, barely holding on, but knowing that if the string was cut, I would be set adrift permanently, never able to find my way back through the hole to myself.

"Where would I be if I let go?" asked the me outside.

"Don't let go. It's too hard to get back," came my answer.

Surely, I did not need any more challenges!

So, I would lie down on the couch, close my eyes, and repeat:

I am in a safe place.

I am not lost.

I will be okay.

I just need rest.

After resting and clearing my mind, I found I could wake up and be back in my house, breathing normally. That was reassuring. It was healing, taking its own time.

There were times after falling through that hole, though, when I was out of my mind. Most often, they would be brief.

I would be aware they had happened and would quickly crawl back into my reality sphere and reassure myself that I could stay there. But there were two times when I was "out there" that I vividly remember not being able to find my way back. I now refer to these times as "when I was crazy."

Patients of mine have sometimes confided that they were terrified they were losing their minds because of the trauma of a loss or depression, and they feared they would be overcome and unable to return to normal. They would whisper the word "crazy," then look around as if someone would hear them and lock them up in an asylum.

It was with great assurance that I could whisper back, "I have been there, and I can guarantee you will come back. It may take longer than you want, but you will return to reality. You just had a little break from it, that's all."

It is because of the following stories I could reassure them that if they "went crazy," they would come back.

Some guy I had never met before showed up at my door a few times and demanded money from me that he said Kerry had owed him. I don't remember much about the first two times he came, but I do recall telling him I had no idea who Kerry owed money to and that I had no control over his money anyway. He should take it up with the probate lawyer handling Kerry's case.

When I heard him pounding on my door on the morning of the third time he came by, I was pissed. He may have woken me up after a twenty-four-hour shift at the hospital, or not. But when I saw his black pickup in the driveway through the kitchen window, I slipped my snub-nosed .38 Special revolver into the right-hand pocket of the pink terry-cloth robe I was wearing.

We spoke through the latched screen door.

He yelled about some work he had done for Kerry and that he needed the money now.

"Look," I said, "you are not getting the point, and I am sick of telling you to not come here again." I took the revolver out and held it in my two hands, not pointing it at him, just showing it to him. "So, I am telling you for the last time. Don't show your face around here again. I am not in my right mind, and I honestly don't know what I'll do if I get angry."

Suddenly, I could see the whites of his eyes as he backed slowly away and then turned and ran to his truck. I felt a little bad about flashing the .38, but I wanted to get him out of my life. And he sure grasped the part about my "not being right."

Not my proudest moment, yet I didn't care. I was in survival mode. And it worked. He never came back.

There was something about my grief that taught me to be intolerant, to not take any shit from anyone. All I could think was, *Listen, buddy, I just went through the hellfires of death and near suicide. You have nothing on me. You are a gnat. Bug off.*

Later that day, while sitting at my kitchen desk, I suddenly felt like I was out of my body, seeing myself from across the room. It was like watching a movie of myself with everything in 3D.

I looked down at my hands, turning them over. They looked like mine all right. But it was like I was not connected to them; I couldn't feel them.

Walking around the house, I also couldn't feel my feet touching the floor. I wasn't sure they *were* touching the floor, but looking down, I saw they were there, moving along like they always did.

Back in the kitchen, I sat at my desk and ran my fingers through my hair. From across the room, I could see my hands on the back of my head, and I didn't feel that either.

Time to call for help, I thought. *Who would be home in the middle of the day? Maureen works from home. I could try her.*

When she answered the phone, I said, "Maureen, I can't tell where my body begins and ends. It's scaring me."

"Where are you?" Maureen asked.

"I am sitting at the desk in my kitchen, but I am not solidly here," I replied. "I feel like I am sitting in a theater watching a movie of myself. It's been like this for a while now, and it's not going away. Can you come up here and check on me?"

"I can't get up to you right now," she said. "Do you think you could drive down here to Pasadena?"

"I guess so." Would I be watching myself on the highway outside the car at sixty-five miles an hour?

"Can you drive?" (Why is she asking me that?)

"I think I can. I seem to be on some kind of autopilot." I looked in the garage. The car seemed normal.

"Okay," Maureen said. "Get in the car and see if you feel okay. If not, call me back."

Somehow, the movie theater experience stopped, and I pulled out of the driveway like I always did. I reached Maureen and Gary's, but I don't remember any of the drive. It was like I was willing myself to be there, and the next thing I knew, I was in their house. Hugging Maureen felt like someone dying of thirst getting a drink of water, but my body still did not feel like it usually did.

There are two things I remember finding very helpful. First, Maureen suggested I take a long, hot shower, which felt amazingly good. As I washed my whole body, it started to feel as if it were *mine* again.

I'd been through the fire of personal devastation, the air of disembodiment, and now the magical soul nourishing of water. I knew that the grounding of earth was soon to follow. These four natural elements are powerful.

Second, Maureen told me, "You are having dinner with us and spending the night." What a relief! I don't think I could have driven home that night, anyway. I had used up whatever energy I had to get there.

After dinner, Maureen said, "You are sleeping with us." They didn't have a spare bed.

"Where?"

"In our bed."

"In your bed? Where are you guys going to sleep?!"

"With you. Gary and I are making a Marianne sandwich tonight." Maureen said it like she and Gary had decided it was essential.

Though shocked at first, I was in no position to argue. We all piled into their bed. All night, I was hugged by one or the other of them, and sometimes both. The warm bodies, the pure outflow of love, the contact and the connection could not have been more right.

Waking the next morning, I felt better than I had in months. My body was my own again, with all my parts connected—even my mind.

After a delicious big breakfast, I drove home and remembered the entire drive. Yippee! I never had that severe out-of-body experience or loss of body definition again. Thank God, and thank Maureen and Gary.

Looking back, I recognize the incredible power of friendship—of those people who know and care for you when you need it the most. Who knows how long it would have taken me to come back from wherever those traumas sent me without the unconditional love showered on me by Maureen and Gary? Friends are miracles in life, or at least angels. We all need them and hopefully we'll have the opportunity to *be* them too.

The idea of becoming sensory deprived obviously had not crossed my mind. After months of physical contact with Kerry, being cut off must have been like being an addict in withdrawal. I needed my fix, and without it, I was coming apart.

From then on, I found I could get my contact fix by spooning on the rug with my malamutes. They loved rolling around, receiving cuddles and attention. Sometimes, I could even get a legit Marianne sandwich.

This experience taught me to advise patients who seemed sensory deprived to sign up for a massage or ask someone to give them one. It could be as simple as rubbing their feet. But our bodies crave contact, and after a shock, we each need special attention in our own ways.

Months later, when I was experiencing more normalcy in my life, I decided to go to a medical conference in Los Angeles. My doctor brain was working well, and the event would ensure that I was up to date on current practices. I signed up and looked forward to getting out of town.

At the conference registration desk, I chatted with a nice, young, twenty-something man as he handed me the forms to fill out. "Where are you working? When did you graduate?" The usual questions, but then he asked, "What have you been doing since finishing your residency?"

So, I told him the story of meeting Kerry, our connection, the engagement, and the plane crash that killed him on the day we were to pick out our wedding rings. Why did that come out of my mouth?

His face went ashen, and he froze. Then he tried to hide under the tablecloth covering the long registration desk. "Oh, no," he croaked. "I am so sorry." He was talking from under the table.

After that, I heard nothing.

I unraveled and lost focus. My story affecting a stranger like that reinforced the magnitude of Kerry's loss on my own life. The man's reaction threw me, maybe even out of my newfound reality. It was my personal history. Should I have kept it secret?

It was clear I could not sit in a lecture and absorb new ideas at the medical conference. It had been months since I had been out of the Valley. Was there something else I could do while I was in Los Angeles?

Changing gears, I decided to go to a nearby mall and recover my emotional self with some retail therapy. I don't remember driving there or what I bought, but my purchase was in a paper bag leaning against the dressing room wall while I undressed to try on a blouse. That was when a hand came under the door and stole my shopping bag. I quickly threw on my blouse, gathered my things, and charged out of the dressing room hoping to catch the thief. But my package was gone, and there was no way to track it down.

That did it. I was barely keeping it together, and this just sent me over the edge, back to Crazy Land.

Opening my jacket to let my body cool down, I had to remind myself to breathe. Five feet in front of me, I saw a door. I went out through it to an outside balcony and threw my coat on the floor. The sun was shining on a chair.

I sat.

I waited there for a while.

I hummed.

After some time, an employee came, told me the store was closing, and said I would have to leave.

"How do I get out?" I croaked.

She pointed to the door. I went out. Where was I?

Someone directed me out of the building. But how was I going to get home? Who could help me figure things out? I thought about it and then called a few people, but no one answered.

Okay, Marianne, I told myself. *You are lost, and no one is coming to your aid. You are in LA. The store closed, so it must be near rush hour. You will not be able to drive home in that traffic.*

The thought of traffic reminded me that I'd come by car. It had to be parked nearby. Even if I could find it, though, the question remained: what was I actually supposed to do next?

By that time, I had made my quota of decisions for the day, and it seemed clear that no more were coming.

I had to figure out someone to contact. Who did I know in LA that would be home now, after work? There was Maureen and Gary, but they were over in Pasadena. *Too far,* I thought. *Too much traffic. Who else?*

And, like the proverbial bolt from the blue, there was the answer. *Cheryl, my friend from residency. She lives somewhere around here. I used to drive her home sometimes.*

I took out my phone and called her...

"Cheryl, I'm lost." I related the story of the stolen bag, and then the part about "losing it." She understood at once.

"Where are you?" she asked.

Looking around, I walked over to the street sign and read it to her. "I am in West LA, outside Macy's. I think I parked my car in the garage, but I don't know where."

"Okay," said Cheryl. "First, take a deep breath, then walk over to the garage. Take the elevator to the top floor. Start there and walk down, looking at each car. You will find it."

"I will?" I wasn't so sure.

"Yes, you will. Then come to my house. You know the way?"

"Cheryl, I am pretty screwed up right now. Even if you tell me the directions, I don't think I could write them down, follow them, and drive at the same time."

"Okay. Go as far as you remember the way, then call me and I will direct you on the next leg."

After finally finding the car, I congratulated myself on that accomplishment and headed in the direction that I vaguely remembered led toward Cheryl's. I only had to stop twice to call her when I was lost. Well, to be honest, she had to stay on the phone with me while I told her the streets I was on or approaching, and then she told me which way to turn.

Just knowing I was going to see her felt like going on vacation—albeit a mental one. Cheryl's sister had died when they were little, and Cheryl had told me after I lost Kerry about her own history with crazy grief. She listened to my story of the registration guy hiding under the table and my unraveling when the shopping trip had gone bad. She got it.

"People see a beautiful young person and have no idea what that individual is dealing with," she said. How true was that? "It might be better not to tell your story to strangers. You never know how they are going to handle it," she added.

I could understand that. I was in no shape to help that guy deal with his shock over my life.

We sat in her nurturing home and sipped tea in her kitchen, which helped immensely with my anxiety. Then we went out into her garden. Her vegetables looked like a happy parade of green plants waving in the breeze. She explained all her gardening secrets to me, but I bet the most important ingredient in the peace I felt was Cheryl herself.

Next, she picked some of her celery and made fresh celery soup. (I guess that's why I love celery soup to this day!) Between her presence, her garden, and the flavors of that delicious soup, I was back to myself. I was safe inside my bubble again.

After those two experiences of being rescued by trusted friends, I knew that if I was going to get stuck in the fog of my grieving brain and "go crazy," I was also going to come back. It might take time and I might need help, but it would happen.

I also realized that both those significant "lost" times were preceded by another emotional trauma: first, the bill collector and startling us both with my gun, then the guy sliding under the registration table and subsequent theft of my stolen package. Those smaller traumas started emotional avalanches that buried me.

Both times, my sanity was restored by getting help from my friends. Nonjudgmental help. It was pure love. My friends saved me, again and again.

It never ceases to amaze me how important close relationships truly are. So, when you are feeling lost or overwhelmed, don't hesitate to reach out to your friends. You may be surprised by how much they can help ground you again.

Reclaiming the Joy of Cooking

*S*INCE MY COLLEGE DAYS, I have been known for my marinara sauce with either lasagna or stuffed shells. That paired with homemade garlic bread was definitely the basis for that reputation.

I wasn't cooking for anybody after Kerry died, not even myself. I ate most of my meals in the hospital cafeteria, which was not nearly as bad as it sounds. Our small hospital had just been bought from the Seventh-day Adventists. I didn't know a lot about their religion, but the entire kitchen staff had been kept from those days and many were vegetarians. They were great cooks, and everything was fresh and delicious. Honestly, some patients wanted to visit our hospital just because they knew how great our food was.

I went to the grocery store regularly, but just for the staples: bread, milk, eggs, butter and cereal, as well as dog food. Every week, it was the same store, same grocery list. Actually, I didn't even have a list because what I bought never changed. When I wanted something different to eat, I just went to the hospital for lunch or dinner.

After about six months of this, I was wheeling down the grocery aisle with a large bag of dog food in my cart when I saw a box of lasagna noodles midway up on the left-hand shelf. It was right next to the shells. It was as if they'd just shown up. Where had they been all those months? (Right there.) More accurately, where had *I* been? Holy cow!

Somehow, when my mind shut down to protect itself from the trauma of Kerry's crash, there must have been collateral shutdowns. (I now know this is a symptom of a grieving brain.) Here I was, holding onto the shopping cart, staring at pasta boxes in deep thought, trying to comprehend what the heck had happened to my cooking mind. Once again, another area where my brain felt like it had been struck by lightning. I had no idea that could happen to someone.

As I sat in my car in the grocery store parking lot, this conversation played in my head.

LIGHTNING-STRUCK SELF: Man, I am really screwed up!

ENLIGHTENED SELF: No, you *were* really messed up. Now you are coming out of it.

LIGHTNING-STRUCK: It doesn't feel like I am any better.

ENLIGHTENED: Well, you are better, because now you know. Before this, you didn't know.

LIGHTNING-STRUCK: How does knowing you are messed up make you better?

ENLIGHTENED: Because now you have a choice. You
      can continue with parts of your brain shut
      down, or you can revive them.

LIGHTNING-STRUCK: I can?

ENLIGHTENED: Sure. Do you want to cook again?

LIGHTNING-STRUCK: Yeah, I do. I mean I used to
      know how to make my marinara sauce by heart.
      I guess I could do it again.

ENLIGHTENED: There you are, darlin'. Go, girl!

After that conversation with myself, I went back into the store
and bought the ingredients for the sauce and the fixings for
stuffed shells, then headed home.

And as I did so, the conversation continued…

LIGHTNING-STRUCK: Hey, who am I making these
      stuffed shells for?

ENLIGHTENED: It's not *who* you are making them for.
      It's *that* you're making them.

LIGHTNING-STRUCK: Right. (*I got that.*) You know,
      I could make them for myself. (*I laughed.*) I
      could even freeze them.

ENLIGHTENED: There you are. You are coming back.

I felt proud for recouping my lost self. It was like meeting an
old friend.

Crazy Stunts Fueled by Rage

*I*N THE MONTHS after a loved one's death, you may find yourself being tempted to do the craziest things. It can be as if your natural sense of self-preservation shuts down, and your common sense falls victim to the grief and anger you feel, leading you to say and do things you normally wouldn't.

Initially, after Kerry's death, I was in shock. It probably lasted for months. It was like I was crawling around on my hands and knees, trying to figure out how to walk again. Somehow, I had either forgotten how or a ministroke had wiped out that part of my brain responsible for coordination. I almost needed to be led around, or at least given a walker.

I knew death from the inside out. Every cell was affected, especially my brain cells. Maybe people who've undergone electroshock therapy could have related to me, but I didn't even feel like myself.

Some months after Kerry died, I pulled into a gas station after work. At that time, I drove a Nissan 300 ZX sports car. As I neared the gas pump, a truck cut me off. Okay, that can happen innocently enough. So, I pulled around to the second set of gas pumps and the same guy pulled in front of me again. Now I was sure it was intentional.

Once again, I rounded the pumps and stopped right on the other side, opposite the truck that had cut me off. It was one of those dusty desert pickups with a double rifle rack inside across the back of the cab window, and both racks had rifles.

As I inserted the hose nozzle into my tank, I said in a snotty tone over my shoulder, "It wasn't enough to cut me off once, but you had to do it twice."

He said, "You think you own this place, bitch, just because you drive a fancy car?"

"Only if you think you are entitled to be an ass just because you drive a truck."

With that, the face-to-face standoff began. He stepped up on the median to loom over me while he yelled.

I was not having it. I was all in on the fight. Still holding onto the nozzle in my gas tank, I planned to nail him with it if he touched me, as he was threatening to do. We were both yelling at each other, and it felt good for some strange reason.

The next thing I knew, the owner of the gas station was literally standing between us and pushing us apart like a referee in a boxing match. I don't remember if we even got to fill up before he made us both leave.

I was wound up on anger. Maybe it gave me a break from the sorrow. I don't even remember driving home, but I do remember heading back toward the gas station after putting my snub-nosed .38 Special on the passenger seat. There was a stop sign about halfway back to the station.

While I waited at the intersection, I looked at the gun and thought, *What the heck are you going to do with that, girl?* I had no plan, but there was the gun sitting on the seat next to me, loaded with anger.

Are you out of your mind? I asked myself.

Yes, I answered.

Turning around, I headed home. I was shaking uncontrollably. As sweat poured down my sides, the noise of a jackhammer thrumming in my ears was keeping time with my racing heart. Finally, it slowed down. As the anger siphoned off, shame crept in instead.

In the kitchen, I grabbed a beer from the fridge, headed out onto the patio overlooking the valley, and sat at the table. I desperately needed to calm down. All I could feel was my disappointment in my own actions. I had never been so stupid in my life. What was going on with me?

I stared up into the night sky, infinite and unreachable, asking the heavens for help. The next thing I knew, it seemed as though eight-foot orange and yellow flames were coming out of the center of my chest, heading straight up into the sky. Those flames were so real I could feel the heat. They lasted about ten seconds.

Holy shit, I thought. *What was that?* It was the most bizarre thing that ever happened to my body, that's what. Usually, it did what I wanted, but now it was doing unimaginable things.

I waited a few minutes to see what would happen next. More flames? God coming down and striking me dead? I would have deserved it. But nothing happened—nothing at all.

I was in way over my head. I needed to know what those flames were about and how to ensure they didn't return. Who the heck could I call? It's not like you can share "the chest on fire" scenario with just anybody. There is no hotline for "flames shooting out of my body."

I called my best friend Sandy. She had scary crazy stuff in her past that she had shared with me. She would honestly tell me if I was crazy or what. I related the whole evening's events to her, from gas to gun to flames. I confessed my stupidity and my shame.

"But, Sandy," I added. "Those flames… They were so real, and they were scary as all get out. So, tell me the truth. Am I cracking up?"

"No," she replied, "you are not cracking up."

"Thank God! But, Sandy, the flames… The flames were scary real. What were those?"

"Honey," she said, "those flames were rage. You were enraged." The flames had a name. It sounded exactly right. Rage, ragged and roaring.

"Oh my God," I said. "I am enraged and doing scary things." Were there worse things to come? "Now what do I do, Sandy?"

"You get some therapy. Here is my therapist's number. He'll help you."

What I learned from that experience, among many other things, is that you can bury, deny or steel your heart against grief, but you can't make it go away. Sometimes you are too fragile or vulnerable to engage in grieving fully, so you focus on all the other parts of your daily life in order to survive. But someday, somewhere—it could be years later—when the wound is not so fresh and you're not feeling so fragile, the grief or the anger or the overwhelming sadness will come up from wherever it has been stuffed away and demand to be dealt with.

In those first few months after Kerry's death, I guess I had finally gotten over the shock, denial and overwhelming emotions, and now it was time to be serious about my mental health. I needed all the help I could get. I called Sandy's therapist.

Therapy is like cracking open a safe. You suddenly become free.

So, those hours I spent in therapy were beyond helpful. If there is even an inkling that you need support, I highly recommend therapy. Every hour I spent in it was a gift to myself. Understanding where I was in my life and why was essential. Because of that, I had insight into my anger and could make better choices about how I viewed and handled circumstances in the future. I would never have found these by myself. I would probably still be screwed up if I had not worked it all out with my therapist.

I also learned that pain is behind all anger. I knew where mine came from. The trucker would have to do his own inventory, or not. It was up to him.

Pets Grieve Too

*P*ETS ARE CONSTANT COMPANIONS, best friends, walk-takers (over and over), fountains of happiness 24/7, and sources of unconditional love. Sometimes people have a harder time when their pet dies than when a family member does. I have had patients tell me this more than once. I think it has to do with the complete responsibility we feel for the wellbeing of our pets. They depend on us for everything and give us love in return, even if we accidentally step on them. I would never choose to live without a dog in my life.

When Kerry died, I inherited his Alaskan malamute, Magic, who was a year old at the time. He was a magnificent, large, black-and-white malamute who was on his way to being an international champion show dog. After Kerry died, Magic lost weight and became way too thin. His trainer gave me some suggestions about how to deal with his weight loss, but none of them worked.

I heated his food. I cooked steak, chopped meat, and chicken. He would eat if I hand-fed him, but it was painfully slow. I was worried I was going to lose him. After being on the floor in the kitchen for far too many dinners, I actually started to eat my meal while sitting there waiting for him to eat his. Bingo. The weight loss stopped, and as long as I sat on the floor with him, he ate.

The trick was that I had to eat with him. After a few months of eating on the floor together, he in his dog bowl and me with my plate on my lap, he gained his weight back.

We had many conversations there on the kitchen floor, Magic and me. I doubt he cared much about the topics we talked about, but he was a tremendous listener. Over time, he became responsive, energetic, affectionate and playful.

It took me a while to realize that Magic was not grieving Kerry, but connecting to my grief. He was mirroring my sadness. Somewhere over the months after Kerry's death, Magic became *my* dog. He chose me first, and then I chose him as well.

The more love and attention I showered on him, the more attention and love he gave me back. He helped me immensely. I had love back in my life again—a very different love, but love nonetheless. He became the best dog I have ever had.

The more time I spend with dogs, the more I learn about empathy and love.

In the first few years after moving to Connecticut, we had two family dogs. Sam was an eighty-five-pound yellow Lab with light brown eyes and little, black, tented eyebrows he used to move back and forth to express confusion and flatten out when he felt intense joy. Angeline, our twenty-pound, fluffy, white bichon, had a springy jaunt and facial expressions that spoke full sentences of love and contentment.

They were a couple. We have many pictures of the two of them snuggling, but our favorite showed Sam laying on the floor on his stomach, his front paws stretched out in front of him like an Egyptian sphinx, with Angeline's little body draped across his front legs, leaning against his chest—that is, his heart.

Most often, she would sleep like that, and Sam would partially close his eyes, exuding contentment. It was that way daily for years.

When Sam died, I wondered how we could communicate to Angeline what had happened. Perhaps if she could see his dead body, she would understand? Actually, I was more worried about Angeline's reaction than about my own. After smelling Sam, though, she slowly backed away, tail hanging low. It was all I could do to let her know why he was gone, why he would not be there for her anymore.

After that, Angeline's tail never curled up like it used to. It was worse than seeing a flag at half-mast. When we went for walks, her tail hung down between her hind legs, lifeless and dragging on the ground. She walked around the house like she was lost. It was torture to see, and everyone commented on it. Every part of her seemed to be grieving.

I knew a dog could smile, but not that a dog could look so heartbroken. After seeing that sad face staring at me as I drove out of the driveway to work a few times, I started taking her with me. It was little help, but at least she was not alone. She moped around the office, often sitting outside the room where I saw my patients.

Meanwhile, my daughter Caitlin was living alone during her second year at college and was having a tough time with the Colorado winter. Maybe it was seasonal depression or maybe she was just low on joy in her life, a rare experience for Caitlin. Either way, Angeline came to the rescue.

She went to live with Caitlin, who took her to the park and on walks several times a day. They both improved, what with the company and extra exercise. Angeline started holding her tail up again! But I must say, to the critical eye, it was never quite as curly as it had been when she was with Sam.

Caitlin and Angeline finished college together, and also medical school and residency. When it was Angeline's time to die, many tears were shed, but I honestly felt that she reconnected with Sam. The thought of them together again helped all of us with her loss.

We animal lovers know the intensity of love that comes from our pets, which may have greater significance to us than from many people we know. It follows that their love and spirit would also continue in an afterlife. Why would they be left out?

The dogs I have loved and lost are still in my heart. I miss them. When I die, I want to go to "dog heaven" because I want to be with them almost as much as with anybody else I've lost. What a glorious reunion that would be! I could be licked, romped on, and sandwiched in the spiritual realm, however that might happen. Yes, that would be my ideal heaven!

Lately, thanks to Justine, I have also met some amazing cats. Maybe there is room for more animal love in my life…

Part IV. Firsts Without

Celebrating Special Occasions

*T*HE FIRST YEAR WITHOUT YOUR LOVE one will be challenging, especially during special occasions like birthdays, anniversaries and the holidays. You may wonder how you can hold onto your loved one's memory and also continue to enjoy family events without them. The answers lie within you. Some grievers continue to do things the way they have always been done, and some change things up. You may have friends sing or tell stories of how you all celebrated together. Or you could cook your loved one's favorite food in their honor or include them in a blessing said before the meal.

It doesn't have to be a time of intense sadness even if a few tears are shed. The place your loved one held in your heart will always be there, it's just the pain of losing them that diminishes with each passing year, not your love for them.

We knew that the first Thanksgiving without Thom was going to be rough. So, the girls and I ran away, hoping to escape the pain of Thom's absence. We flew to California to be with my sister and then my cousin Mary Ann—two of my most powerful supporters.

Everyone was feeling festive, except for Caitlin, Justine and me. It was like being from another country, another culture, another world. We knew we were going to have Thanksgiving without Thom, but to not have Thom *and* not have the comfort of our home made it seem like we were in some alternate universe.

What I mostly remember is thinking, *What is happening here? This is awful. We are with people who love and care for us, but I feel like throwing up.*

There were too many of us in Regina's tiny Pasadena house, so we were all eating on TV trays. Instead of the cool brisk weather of a New England fall, it was hot and everyone was in shorts. It felt like Thanksgiving in July.

Justine whispered to me insistently, "Mom, what are we doing here? This is too weird."

I think she wanted to say more, but she was being polite.

Our first Christmas without Thom was going to be difficult too. It was his favorite holiday. He got to cook all his favorite meat dishes, sauces and gravies, and they were delicious. His Christmas light decorating talents knew no bounds. Each year, he would drag the knot of last year's lights down from the attic, hang them up, and then go to the store for a few more strings. Small white lights were his forte.

On Thanksgiving weekend, he tackled the porch railing and the gutters over the front and side doors first, then he moved on to the evergreen trees outside. It wasn't garish, just plentiful.

Inside, the Christmas tree twinkled white, as did the railing between the girls' bedrooms upstairs. The only departure from the white lights were the strings around the copper exhaust fan over the cook top. Those had little red plastic chili pepper covers on them, which emitted a warm red glow to his entire cooking area. He was in his glory. Our electric company loved him.

Choosing a Christmas tree in Connecticut was quite different from doing so in the desert. In California, trees that had been cut and tied already were shipped down from the Pacific Northwest. Then they were neatly stacked according to height in an empty lot in town. We always chose the tallest one that we could squeeze into the living room, as evidenced by the green streaks along the seven-foot-high ceiling.

Getting a tall tree in Connecticut was a new challenge. We had a twenty-foot ceiling in our great room. Talking Thom down to a fifteen-foot tree was the best I could do.

Very unlike the desert, Connecticut has a lot of Christmas tree farms to pick from. You could even pick out your tree, cut it down yourself, and put it in your house the same day. The hardest part was picking the correct tree height. Amazingly, the same tree looks significantly smaller on the farm than it does in your living room. The proof lies in the number of times you have to drag the tree in and out of the house to cut off yet another foot of the trunk.

Tall, recently cut trees in a big picture window not only drink a lot of water, but they also reach toward the light. Two years in a row, we found our tree waking us up in the middle of the night by crashing down and breaking most of our ornaments.

Therefore, the second year, I asked Thom, "Don't you think we should somehow stabilize the tree?"

"Oh, no. I did a much better job of tightening the bolts on the trunk this year."

That night… *crash*.

The third year, I bought screw eyes and heavy fishing line and secured the tree at three points to the molding over the corner windows. We were able to sleep through the night undisturbed.

I was determined that, unlike the first Thanksgiving without Thom, the first Christmas would be as close as possible to those in our past, albeit not as well-lit. Off to the Christmas tree farm we went, and in record time, we had our tree cut down. It was a little smaller than previous trees, but still pretty tall.

My feeling of accomplishment was short-lived, however. The farmer asked who was going to help carry the tree in and put it in the stand. Looking at my eight- and thirteen-year-old girls, it was obvious they would not be strong enough. Why hadn't I thought about that?

The friendly farmer was quick to grasp the situation and asked his grandson to help us out.

"See," I said to myself, "there is a God who looks after widows."

He got the tree in the stand. The girls and I set up our thirteen-foot, blue metal ladder, and then I secured the tree to the screw eyes left in place from the previous year. With Justine looking on, Caitlin and I managed to untangled the lights and put them on the tree, then mounted the pink chiffon angel on top.

By this time, my forearms were a mess of hives! Since Thom had always taken tree-light duty, I never knew I was allergic to Douglas fir tree needles. But after slathering on some steroid cream, I could still enjoy the beauty of the deep forest green tree with twinkling white lights and the scent of pine in the air, all imparting a special holiday spirit.

Next, it was time to haul the ornaments down from the attic. By the time I'd gone up and down those stairs a few times, I was exhausted, like I had run a marathon. Each box felt ten times heavier than it should have. (It seems emotional weight doesn't register on a scale.)

Opening the boxes of ornaments had me rapidly reviewing each Christmas with Thom. "Baby's first Christmas" ornaments for each girl, the ones they made at school, pictures of them with toothless grins, special ornaments we had bought together, ornaments from trips we took… Suddenly, the delightful setting before me blurred. All I could see was what was not there. Thom.

There seemed to be some vital essence draining out of my soul. I was melting. The work was done, but I was undone.

While the girls were enjoying the ornaments, I was propped up with pillows on the couch in an effort to reconstitute my mind and body. While I drank an entire bottle of water, I thought about how I could not keep kidding myself. We were not still the happy family we had been when Thom was alive. *Okay. Get a grip*, I told myself.

The feeling that something essential was missing had been under the surface since Thanksgiving. Even at the office, hundreds of cards equated happy holidays with pictures of families—Mom, Dad and kids, all with smiling faces in front of Christmas trees, some even with their dogs. Magazine covers in the waiting room and exam rooms proclaimed how to make your holidays merry and bright, with delicious meals for "the whole family."

That was not happening at my house. What about the rest of us? How about the grieving families? What about the recently divorced ones and the others who were not completely whole? How were they doing? It's funny that pain can give you insight into suffering in a way you never knew existed, nor wanted to know.

Somehow, I had to shift from that negative state, return to the here and now, and be grateful for the beauty there in our living room. As I looked around, what should appear to my wondering eyes but my nine-year-old Justine.

She was gleefully picking out her favorite ornaments from each box and had already placed her horse ornaments, pictures of herself, and her favorite wind-up toy ornaments on the tree. In her hand, she held a small fluffy sheep made of real wool, wearing a tiny leather collar with a sprig of holly under the chin. She tenderly attached it to the tree. Since she was not allowed on the ladder, she was dressing the tree from her tippy-toe height of six feet down to the lowest branches. In some weird way, the scene was beautiful—her part of the tree with its ornaments aglow in the white twinkling lights.

Then she took out the Christmas tree skirt. "Oh, Mom," she rejoiced, "this is my favorite." She donned the green velvet skirt bordered in red satin ribbon and covered with ornaments made of red, gold and silver sequins, putting it around her own thin waist and attaching the Velcro.

Caitlin put on the music from The Nutcracker's "Dance of the Sugar Plum Fairy," and Justine twirled around until she became dizzy and fell down. All three of us were in fits of the giggles.

I was back.

Several months before, I had bought the girls' Christmas presents and hid them in Thom's closet. Then, three weeks before Christmas, I searched the house but couldn't find those gifts. Perhaps I had dreamed that I bought them? Remember, I was operating with a "grief brain" here.

Grief brain is different from a normal brain in which all the parts are connected. A grief brain has tiny little holes in it like Swiss cheese, where the connections are broken. You don't know where the holes are until you hit a disconnect. My memory seemed to be the most affected. I came to accept those disconnects as part of the grieving process. (Did I really do something or did I just plan to do it?)

Not sure whether I had presents, I bought more of them, including an English saddle for Justine's future horse. After wrapping the gifts, I went to hide them in Thom's closet… And there were all the other presents. So I wrapped those too. What the heck?

The most fun I had in months was watching those girls open that mountain of presents. I told them the story of the lost gifts, which made them laugh. We then sat in the middle of a mound of discarded wrapping paper, eating milk chocolate candy from the Christmas stockings. Thank God we made it through.

As we relaxed in the great room on our green and purple velvet couches, I gazed over at the tree and was surprised by two things. First, the tree was dressed with ornaments only on its lower half—as far up as Justine could reach. Second, the blue metal ladder was still there from weeks before, when Caitlin and I had put the lights on.

What an odd combination: a thirteen-foot blue ladder next to a half-dressed tree! All the nights that I'd plugged in the tree lights, I had never noticed either. (More grief brain disconnects?)

I looked over at Caitlin and Justine, popping chocolates into their mouths with their slippered feet resting on the big, round, oak coffee table filled with presents. Caitlin leaned over and gently elbowed her sister in her side. She pointed to all the presents and said, "Justine, this grief thing is working out in our favor."

We have told that story many times since, and it just gets funnier with each telling.

What I learned from those first holidays as a single parent was that as precious as memories sometimes are, they can constrain my expectations, wanting everything to be like it always was. Sometimes, we need to be open to new expressions of special occasions.

Years ago, a friend of mine lost her fiancé unexpectedly. She was feeling low on his first birthday after his death. Two significant things happened to her that day.

In the morning, friends from church came over to spend time with her. They talked and prayed with her, mourning her loss and joining her in her grief. The time spent together was heartfelt and greatly appreciated, but when they left, my friend somehow felt sadder than she had earlier in the day.

Later that afternoon, she answered a knock at her door to find another friend standing on her front porch with a fistful of balloons in one hand and a birthday cake in the other. They put candles on the cake and sang "Happy Birthday." Together, they celebrated her fiancé's life and the love they had shared. She tells me that as odd as it felt, it truly raised her spirits and made a difficult day that much easier.

This story illustrates how there can be very different attitudes about grieving. Mourning the death of a loved one doesn't have to meet others' expectations. It may involve weeping or celebration. Grieving is an acknowledgment of the significance of a deep connection between two hearts and minds. Love transforms us so life is worth living and love is worth the cost of grieving.

If you can get to a place of feeling grateful for what you have had in your life, it can really help you live and take part in the present. New experiences may be added to or replace old ones and that is okay.

Once you accept that things will be different, it permits you to define a new "normal" that brings you joy.

Firsts Without Your Love

*W*E CRIED, laughed and emotionally limped through the holidays and birthdays in those first months. Next on the "Firsts without Thom" list would be our summer vacation. The four of us had been tried-and-true campers. Every summer, we were off for two weeks of swimming, biking and campfires in New England, mostly in Vermont. We always stayed one night in a bed-and-breakfast as a special treat.

Contemplating two weeks' camping without Thom, I choked up. If I could dress only half a Christmas tree and leave a thirteen-foot ladder in my living room without even noticing it for weeks, I could only imagine what I might miss, trying to pull off a camping trip on my own.

The one good thing about our weird Thanksgiving escape to California was that on the plane on the way home, I thumbed through the airline magazine tucked in the seat pocket in front of me. There was an article about rafting down the Colorado

River through the Grand Canyon. Now that would be *the* place to go camping. It was one of my favorite destinations. Not only would we be camping in one of the most gorgeous locations in the world, but the clincher for me was that I would have help.

When I got home, I made reservations with an Arizona river company that had huge pontoon rafts. In July, the girls and I would traverse the Grand Canyon from start to finish.

Here is how I told the girls. "Summer is coming. We are going to make a slight departure from our usual trip to Vermont."

As I explained the plan to go rafting for a week, sometimes in flat water but sometimes in Class V rapids (the most thrilling rapids around), I heard little squeals of joy and excitement from both the girls as they hopped from one foot to the other. No, they were not sad to give up the Vermont trip. They probably knew I couldn't pull it off.

"Your dad is dead," I said. "But *we*," I continued, pointing to the three of us, "are definitely *not* dead." Heads nodded in agreement. "And *we* are going to have *fun*."

At that, their eyebrows flew up, and they hugged each other, jumping up and down. "Go, Mom. Go, Mom!" they chanted.

A well-needed home run. I congratulated myself on picking a vacation that would work well for all of us.

The week on the Colorado was prefaced by three days in Las Vegas. Now *there* is a place where your normal world is suspended. We spent each day in the "here and now." The streets and people were almost as much fun as the shows. Justine especially enjoyed *Blue Man Group*, and Caitlin and I thought the music in *Mamma Mia!* was awesome.

After the three days in Las Vegas, we were bused over to the beginning of the Colorado River—from wild noise and neon lights to quiet and tranquil nature. There was no time to be sad. (Or to cook!) Everything on the packing list they sent us went into dry bags, and then we were on the raft and in the water. It was exciting to find that we had a geologist on our raft. The trip turned out to be the best history and geology lesson ever.

About the third night out, we were camped on a small beach. Justine insisted on sleeping in the tent despite the heat because the previous morning she'd had a scorpion on her life vest. She felt safer in the tent.

Somehow, the creepy crawlies didn't bother Caitlin or me. We were on the sand outside the tent, lying on our sleeping pads with wet sheets over us that had been dipped in the river and wrung out to keep us cool at night. It was an almost cinematic moment, with the blue-black sky cast with a million brilliant stars and the Milky Way slung midway between the ocher canyon walls on either side of us. The view was literally breathtaking.

After some time, Caitlin said, "Mom, this is the most beautiful thing I have ever seen." She spoke with a large sigh and the release of something bottled up for far too long.

"I feel it too, honey. It's like nature is reminding us of all the beauty out there to enjoy."

"Mom, thanks for taking us on this trip. We're having so much fun."

"Me too, my love."

Caitlin and I held hands as we lay watching nature unfurl her star-spangled banner. It was impossible for us to close our eyes and sleep, or even talk. Sometime later, we watched the moon rise in slow motion over the eastern canyon wall. As it came up on the left, it cast a glow on the right-hand wall of the canyon, like a moonrise in stereo. It was a full moon, broadcasting beauty. And our hearts were at peace.

For the first time in a long while, the weight of being a widow, of being a single mom, of getting on with life lifted. The Grand Canyon and Colorado River washed my troubles away.

Surrounded by nature at its best, I felt uplifted and positive about our future. I could do it. The grip of grief was lessening. I really would be okay. The girls would be okay. We would not be looking back anymore. We would look forward. That trip, that night, being with my girls, the healing connection, and the wonder of nature has never left me. It has been a lifelong, happy thought.

Getting out into nature can be so restorative. Patients have often told me that a few hours at the beach (even in winter) can add significantly to the healing process. Try it!

Here is what helps when navigating your firsts without your loved one. Stay focused on the gratitude you feel for being able to be present while you participate in life's events. Just by staying in the here and now, you are being present in the moment, which enables you to focus on something other than your worries and fears. Sharing time together with those you love will help you feel connected to people, places and nature again, and your brain will be bathed in calming hormones that adjust your attitude positively.

When Grief Sneaks Up on You

THREE YEARS AFTER THOM DIED, Caitlin was a senior in high school. She and I had a list of college open houses to attend. At each one, she was able to check out the campus, the teachers, the dorms, the food and the vibe. Could she see herself there for the next four years?

We were on our way to her first open house when we stopped at a gas station to fill up and Caitlin got a cup of coffee. She set it on the floor between her feet, and as she leaned across to pull on her seat belt, she accidentally kicked it over. My anger went from zero to sixty in one second flat.

"Caitlin, what the hell were you doing leaving the top off the coffee? What were you thinking? Look at the mess you made!" I screeched. "What's the matter with you?"

One glance at Caitlin's crestfallen face told me how inappropriate my anger was. There was my beautiful, hope-filled daughter, suddenly devastated. It was supposed to have been an exciting mom-and-daughter weekend! Why did I do that?

"Oh, Caitlin… I am so sorry. I didn't mean that at all. It's just coffee. We can clean it up." With that, I burst into tears. "That is not even what I am angry about, honey."

Seeing her confusion, I said, "Somehow I always looked forward to this day, anticipating the choices of your bright future. I thought it would be the three of us: you, me and Dad. This day—it was a dream I had for you… for us. What I am really angry about is that he is not here for all the excitement. I didn't even realize this was going on inside me. The anger over the coffee just connected me to it. And I took it out on you. I am so sorry."

"It's okay, Mom. I get it." I handed her the tissues, and we blew our noses in stereo. "I miss him too." Her tears left a trail on her face and two dark spots on her raincoat.

I regrouped. "Well, he is not here, and I will not let that fact ruin our great weekend. Honey, go back in there and get two more coffees, one for you and one for me. Let's start over."

This set the tone for a wonderful trip. She was refocused, and with that, she cranked up some great tunes on the radio and we headed down the road, both somewhat lighter than before.

Even though life goes on and we eventually resume some semblance of normalcy, we never truly get over grief. It may not be a constant companion, but it can rear its head at the most unexpected times.

When Thom was dying, we spoke about all the events in the girls' lives that he would miss: the graduations, the days their braces came off, the weddings, the grandchildren he would never see. I thought I grieved then for our unrealized future. I also thought that talking about it at that point would save me from the disappointment of it when the time arrived, but I could not have foreseen the smaller milestones that spouses usually share.

After this episode with Caitlin, I made a mental note to anticipate these events that he should have been there for, and then try to address the anger before it took control.

When those special days arrived, it still hurt, but the anger was in check. I was really proud of myself for being mindful of my feelings, so when it came time for me to walk Caitlin down the aisle on her wedding day, I could celebrate her and celebrate with her—without Thom.

It's funny how grief from your past can sabotage the present. Knowing that can happen doesn't always prevent it.

If you find yourself drawn back to painful grief, acknowledge how you're feeling and then try to let it go. Remind yourself that the hurt was in the past. You can diminish its impact if you reflect on how far you have come in learning to live with your grief.

Anniversary Reaction

MY OFFICE MANAGER, Wendy, chuckles whenever I refer to her as "my office wife." After working together for twenty-five years, we have spent the vast majority of our weekdays with each other—not only working together but caring for the needs of our patients (our work family) and each other. We also went through a fair amount of grieving together: my mom, her dad, my husband Thom, her sister.

The caring and support we shared made it possible to survive our losses with a minimal amount of trauma at work. We reminded each other to eat, sleep and laugh.

I could count on Wendy for almost anything. She had a "down home" kind of attitude with an abundance of common sense, which I valued greatly. (It's surprisingly hard to find these days.)

Our teamwork was legendary for those patients who knew us well. Sometimes, they would come in to see her, not me.

She was the first person I saw each morning, and the last person each night. Often, I felt she was an extension of me. In contacting patients, she literally was; they often relied on her care as much as my own. We were an awesome team. Really! The thing I miss most in retirement is Wendy.

She called me one day. For the past two weeks, she'd been going to bed at 8 p.m., sleeping late, and taking a long nap each day. At first, she couldn't figure out what was wrong. She didn't have a fever or cough, and she didn't feel sick. Then she thought back to something I taught her over the years: continued fatigue without explanation is most often depression.

Depression, even a mild one, is a heavy emotional burden. It feels like you are dragging a ball and chain around, which is exhausting. It's no wonder a depressed person feels tired.

Wendy told me she was sad about her brother-in-law's dying a few weeks before. Then the anniversaries of all the other family deaths around that time of year triggered even more pain. Her father, her stepmother and both her sisters, years apart... They all felt like they had just happened, affecting her unconscious mind first.

Even though these deaths had occurred years ago, the combined grief exhausted her. She realized this was why she was so tired. It's possible that, now that she was retired, she didn't have the daily distractions to keep her thoughts from dwelling on those she'd lost and was re-grieving their deaths.

We never really finish grieving. A new death somehow reminds you of a previous one, and then the sadness from one bleeds over onto the other like a watercolor painting. They are all connected. Say Bill dies, and there we are at his funeral, feeling sad about losing him. Next thing we know, we are crying about our dead mother. Wherever our grief hides, it is a swirling mix of emotions. Most often, it remains under our emotional radar, but certain situations can reach in there, pull up one of those feelings, and demand that you grieve some more.

Grief has its own control valve and knows no bounds. It wants you to come to terms with your loss. So it pokes its head up when you least expect it, reminding you that what you had is no more.

Feelings that resurface at a certain time of year have a name: anniversary reaction. Although I learned about them in my studies, I never really understood them until I met Linda.

Linda became my patient when she moved into an extended care facility in our town. She was in pretty good shape for an eighty-year-old. Her primary problem was dementia, and her poor memory made it unsafe for her to live alone.

One April day, Linda came in with a classic case of shingles all along her right side. She was treated and got better, and all was well until the next April, when she came in again with another case of shingles.

Having shingles a second time, again in April, was no coincidence. What was special about the month? Her caregivers denied any unusual stress or illness, or even contact with anyone with chickenpox or shingles. What came out in that interview was that five years earlier, her husband had died in April. Here was a lady with dementia who could barely remember her husband—but her body remembered. Linda was proof that there is such a thing as "body memory," which lives independently of our consciousness.

Who knows what triggers these memories? It could be a seasonal celebration or song or food, or the way the sunlight angles through the trees at a certain time of year. But your body knows.

During the week in early December when Thom and I had our wedding anniversary, which also includes my mother's and grandmother's birthdays, I get migraine headaches, every year. Even though I am now happily remarried, those headaches just keep coming back.

Somehow, I never remember it's about to happen, until recently. I knew that sucker was coming and told Gene, "This first week in December is always a rough one for me, so I could use some extra tender care."

In anticipation, I did relaxing things. I made sure my stress level was low and remembered times with Thom and Mom and Nana. The migraine still came, but only for one day! Yippee! I felt I was gaining on it.

Maybe awareness of important milestones can change your reaction. But even if it cannot, it can at least explain some physical symptoms or short-temperedness around that time of year.

Practice good self-care by avoiding adding any more stress to your life around significant anniversary dates.

The Double-Edged Sword

*P*HYSICIANS KNOW how important a person's family history is in guiding us when scheduling their preventive care. One day, a woman I will call "Jill" came in for her yearly physical exam. Her sister had died of breast cancer, so I reminded her to schedule her mammogram soon.

Immediately, her entire demeanor changed. Her voice hardened, her mouth drew into a tight grimace, and as she spoke about her sister, she was almost spitting with anger.

"That never should have happened. She was only in her forties when she got breast cancer. She lost so much weight, I could hardly look at her." Now Jill was in tears. "She was in so much pain. The whole thing just made my blood boil."

"It sounds awful." I reached for the tissues.

"It's so hard to see someone you love so physically reduced." The intensity of her emotions made me feel like it had just happened.

"Jill, when was this?"

"Three years ago, but it feels like yesterday. I'm still so pissed off. It wasn't supposed to be this way." She blew her nose.

This was definitely a moment that called for a big hug. She melted into my arms. As I held her, I contemplated how she hadn't accepted her loss yet, even after all this time.

It is difficult to experience a family member's death, especially when they are not old. Jill was obviously close to her sister, but the anger was still so raw. How could I help her resolve that a bit before it ate her up? As a physician, I know that mental stress has such significant physical repercussions, in addition to what it was already doing to her mental state.

We spoke about what it is like for the dying person, as well as their family. I shared how all three of my daughters felt that if their dad had to die, cancer was better than just dropping dead. It gave them time to tell him so many things during the goodbyeing.

But Jill still did not see it. "At least if she'd dropped dead, it wouldn't hurt so much."

"I understand," I said, thinking back to what it was like to see my athletic husband become a bald, eighty-pound invalid. An image of him at the end flashed in my mind's eye. His sunken eyes, his temples slightly caved in, his fingers like pale, skin-covered bones.

"You know, it's weird," I said, "but when my husband lost his hair and about one hundred pounds, his pathetic physical self was what convinced me he had to die. He obviously could not go on the way he was. He had given it his best shot. Nothing was working. Watching that process, as heartbreaking as it was, instilled in my core that unconscious knowledge. I helped me to let him go."

She nodded as she looked down at the floor. Perhaps the idea was taking hold that a slow death could be better than her sister dropping dead.

Then I said something that surprised her. "Some people say that the process of wasting away, dying slowly, right before your eyes… It is their gift to you." I paused as she looked up. "The wasting away tells you in no uncertain terms that they are dying. It is out of their control. They have to leave you. It is giving you a chance to say your farewells and thank them for being in your life. As painful as it is, it is your last chance— the chance to balance their loss with gratitude for their being here at all. But it is a chance that not everyone gets. For my kids, that made all the difference."

At this point, Jill looked a little shell-shocked. "You're kidding, right?" she asked as if this was completely new to her. "If you say so." She paused. "I'll think about it."

Jill needed to know that pain didn't make it wrong. It means you had someone worth the pain of grieving. Grief is a consequence of love. Every lament is a love song in disguise.

The next time I saw Jill, we reviewed her mammogram, which was negative. We spoke of her sister, and I asked, "How are you doing with the grief?"

"I am still working on it," she said, with less anger in her voice, no face-tightening and no spitting. She looked at me with a smirking sideways glance, like we shared a secret. Maybe we did. Her attitude was, I am in the middle of anger, trying to tame it and let it go, little by little, trying to find a bit of peace with it all.

Part V. Moving On

Regina and Dating

After my brother-in-law Ken's death, I kept close contact with my sister Regina. She was in her fifties, living alone in their small house in Pasadena. Her only daughter, Lee, was living in Nevada. While talking, FaceTiming and texting are great, you feel the loss of a good partner most when you are all alone.

It was months after Ken died when I got a tearful phone call from Regina. "Marianne, I am so lonely, I can't stand it. At work, I am okay, but I dread coming home at night. Even being with the dog is not helping how lonely I feel. Before I met Ken, I spent twenty years as a single mom. Somehow, it was easier to be alone then. Lee was at school, but not too far away. Now Lee is in Nevada, and I miss her more too.

"What I miss the most about Ken are the simple things we did together: sharing meals, taking walks, going down to the sailboat each weekend, working on the boat together." Her voice cracked. "The little everyday things that were so much fun to share."

At this point, I had been widowed for about twelve years and understood the smothering loneliness.

"Yeah, I hear you," I said. "Working on a shared passion can be such a meaningful form of communication."

"That's it. That is what I miss so much." Regina blew her nose. "My tolerance for being alone is just about zero right now. So, I want your opinion about something. Do you think it would be too soon for me to start dating?"

"Too soon?! Too soon for who? Too soon to want to enjoy life again? Listen, Regina, no one knows better than the two of us how quickly life can end and take your joy with it. If you are worried about what other people think or say, then ignore them as best you can. If they have a negative attitude about it, not only do they not know loss, but they are not your friend."

"Yeah, but I thought it might be too soon. I really don't know what I'm supposed to do."

"Gina, if you feel like having some company, adult conversation, dating… go for it. You had years alone before Ken. You and he were a great match. So maybe that makes being alone now more intolerable. You don't want to go back to being alone. You want to share your time with someone. I get it. Bring some enjoyment back into your life, Gina." I heard some sniffles. "If you have the energy and want to go out for dinner, a walk or anything else that feels good, do it. I mean, really… Why not? Life is for the living. I know I will be thinking how smart my sister is for finding something to bring joy back into her life. This means you are ready. I want you to be happy."

"Thanks. I needed that."

As I think back to this conversation with my grieving sister, it occurs to me that, in generations past, widows wore black and felt and acted sad for a prescribed amount of time. But this was the 21st century. These ideas about how a widow "should" act are definitely out of date. No length of time or depth of grief can compare to what you lost. Denying yourself enjoyment doesn't mean you miss your loved one more.

There was also more going on that made Regina feel lonely. Initially, after Ken died, she had many invitations from couples they had socialized with. Over time, these invitations dried up.

I think that after Ken died, she was seen as a threat. Most often, women set the social calendar, and now Regina was not being included in gatherings. She was a good-looking, successful businesswoman in her fifties, and I don't think most people could miss the fact that she was now "available." Being left out by her friends because she was single isolated her even more, which really stung.

She tried the dating scene, but didn't have much luck. This is when she discovered a solution.

Some months after our conversation, Regina met a single guy named Bobby at her boat club. When he was invited out to dinners or parties, he took a female friend with him. He called these friends "plus-ones."

Bobby had a few ladies in his Plus-One Club. He made it clear to them that as much as he loved spending time with them, he was *not* looking for any romantic involvement or an attachment, just good company. This meant that he was never alone at gatherings and dinner parties. What a great idea! No threat, no commitment other than to having fun. No more going to a restaurant with couples and being seated next to the empty chair. (There's nothing like looking at an empty chair to remind yourself you don't have a mate. It can steal your appetite.)

After some time, Regina and Bobby became each other's plus-ones. Together, they did all the boating things that Regina had been missing, and they each had a partner for all their club outings. Over time, they became each other's Only Ones. What a delightful surprise! Love is blooming.

I never really started dating again, but sometimes well-meaning friends tried to "fix me up." I remember when I refused to be fixed up any more. One of my friends set up a dinner date with a guy my age. We met at a local bistro on a Friday night. I wore what I call "sophisticated casual"—slacks, silk blouse and pearl earrings. He wore a Hawaiian cotton shirt, shorts and flip-flops. The flip-flops did me in. The dinner conversation centered on his experience of moving back to his parents' house after his divorce. I was trapped and felt like his therapist.

That was the end of blind dates for me, at least until Marge decided enough was enough...

Marge was the child of a longtime patient of mine. I first met her as a loving, concerned daughter trying to support her aging mother's independence. Her mom had a condo in an adult community in town. Years went by before Marge's mother began the process of dying in her home, like she'd wished, with no more hospitalizations. Eventually, she could no longer get out of bed. Once she was on hospice, I made a few home visits. Soon, she was not eating anymore.

One evening, Marge and I had a simple dinner at her mom's small, round kitchen table with its faded flower tablecloth. We discussed how to proceed with her mom's care at the very end. Those times together, those discussions, helped Marge and I bond.

Some years later, Marge came to the office and asked my receptionist if she could speak to me. She had "a nonmedical" question. It was the end of the day and no one else was in the waiting room. Marge paced as she waited for me. When I entered the room, she stopped pacing and started talking—fast. She was clearly excited about something.

"I have someone I want you to meet."

"Oh, Marge," I said apologetically. "I don't date. The ones I have been on have been disasters."

"No, no! You can't say no!" She was wringing her hands, acting as if this was the worst news she could have gotten.

At last, she slowed down and moved closer to me, took a deep breath, and started over. "This is somebody I worked with for years. Gene is the nicest guy I know. If I wasn't married, I'd be after him."

"Sorry, Marge."

"Listen to me. He is a widower who has his own house, his own job, his own money. He doesn't need you to take care of him, and he's healthy." She was ticking off all the things that could have been issues.

"Sorry."

"I have been after him for two years to ask you out, and now he says he is ready. You can't say no!" Marge certainly knew how to pitch her case. "Look, he has no kids, so there isn't that issue to deal with." She let that sink in. "He is a civil engineer, and he was a helicopter pilot in Vietnam." I had a weakness for pilots and a soft spot in my heart for Vietnam vets—I'd lived through that era too.

Marge saw me weighing all that she had said. I couldn't believe she had gone to all this trouble! There had to be a reason for that. Maybe I should reconsider and check this guy out? He sounded okay. And Marge had addressed all the things that could've been barriers to a good relationship. She ended by saying, "You two are perfect for each other."

"Oh, dear," I said. Did I want to open myself up to someone again? Could I?

"You don't have to do more than go for a cup of coffee," she said cajolingly.

"Okay," I conceded. "If it's a no-go, I'll be out of there in fifteen minutes."

I ended up meeting this man for coffee on—of all things—April Fool's Day! After an hour of talking and laughing, we went out to dinner. Neither of us had an idea about how dating should go at our age, but we figured it out together.

Sometimes, when your acute grieving is mostly behind you, your friends know it before you do. Marge was that friend to Gene. Lucky for me. Lucky for us.

You Will Be Happy Again

The reality is that you will grieve forever.
You will not "get over" the loss of a loved one;
you will learn to live with it. You will heal
and you will rebuild yourself around the loss
you have suffered. You will be whole again,
but you will never be the same. Nor should
you be the same, nor would you want to.

—Elizabeth Kübler-Ross

*W*HEN KERRY DIED, I was taking a course at the University of Southern California medical school one evening a week. My instructor was Steve, a legend at the medical school, known for being an outstanding teacher. He knew about Kerry's death, and after class, he would often invite me into his office to catch up. He knew how grieving worked.

"Steve, when am I going to stop hurting, and when am I going to get over Kerry's death?" I was sure he would have an answer or advice.

"I don't really know, Marianne, but I will tell you a story." Steve shared how his wife of over twenty-five years had actually been a widow when they married. She was a World War II bride. Her first husband had been an airman who flew a bomber. She didn't know where he dropped the bombs, only that he was good at it.

One day, he was out in his plane and his captain called the mission over, but he had a few more bombs left so he went back to drop them. That was when he was shot down and killed.

Steve spoke not only about his wife's devastation but also about how she recovered, how they met and fell in love, and went on to have a family and a full, happy life together. It was encouraging.

"But," he said, "just recently we were planting bulbs together in the yard. We were under a big oak on our hands and knees, bulbs all around, when she sat back and looked at me with tears in her eyes. She asked, 'He had to go back and drop those damn bombs, didn't he?'" He was shaking his head, as if in disbelief at her reconnecting to her grief—or maybe he was sharing in it.

That story was not really the answer I wanted, but it was the story I needed. There was no going back to a place before the pain and no place that would be free of pain going forward. I would have to let it heal over and be okay somewhere inside the new, scarred me. I would be okay. I would.

Life had moved ahead for her, and it would for me too. In time, it will for you as well, my dear.

While you may never get over the fundamental loss of your loved one, you can begin the slow process of learning to live again.

Margaret Atwood, a master writer, says, "There is no plan B. You just have to do it." I like that idea. Recovering, healing, moving on—whatever you call it—is imperative. You have got to do it. Just don't beat yourself up in the process.

If you are holding on to the pain of loss so you can feel connected to the person you lost, think about that. What if you let go of the pain? Does that mean you have to let go of all your wonderful memories? Not at all.

Your loved one surely would not want the most prominent feelings connected with their memory to be pain and sorrow. They are dead. You are not. You are alive and putting your life together. You have a great healing capacity in your heart and mind. It may have been untapped until now, but the fact remains, it is there. It will take time, but you will find it.

Even a broken bone eventually becomes stronger at the break than it was before. This is true. And you will be stronger too. You will.

In the beginning, when you are at ground zero, you may have to take one breath at a time. You must get from one hour to the next, then one day to the next, but you *will* get through. It will be one week, then one month—and you will have made it that far! Each period is a win.

You can do it, little by little. You can choose to believe not only that you are a survivor, but that eventually you will regain happiness in your life. It is out there, don't block it out. It is there for you.

Make your best choices. Be gentle with yourself. You are only human.

How did others who suffered loss get through it? How did they grow from it? What did they do next? Who has stories to share with you to lift your courage and help you power through?

As it turns out, I found examples of grief warriors in the past presidents of the United States! These shortened stories are from Doris Kearns Goodwin, a Pulitzer Prize-winning historian. Here is what I learned from her.

Abraham Lincoln was in his early thirties and struggling with depression and skirting suicide. His best friend said, "Lincoln, you must rally or you will die."

According to Goodwin, Lincoln replied, "I know, and I would just as soon die now, but I have not yet accomplished anything to let any human being know that I have lived." He then ran for the United States Senate twice and for president once—and lost all three times. But in those losses, he gained recognition for his honesty and sterling character, which attracted party leaders to him. In turn, in 1860, they helped him win as a "dark horse" candidate in his second run for president. He won against all odds.

If he had allowed himself to be beaten down by depression or loss, we never would have had the Emancipation Proclamation to abolish slavery. Our nation's history would not be what it is today.

Theodore Roosevelt was twenty-five years old when his wife and mother died, twelve hours apart. He ran away. He spent two years on his ranch in the Dakota territories, mourning the loss of the two most important women in his life. The hours he spent in the saddle each day, driving cattle and hunting big game, gave him a deep appreciation for the incredible healing power of nature.

He eventually went on to become our best conservationist president. He established one hundred and fifty national forests, fifty-one federal bird reserves, four national game preserves, five national parks, and eighteen national monuments on over two hundred thirty million acres of public land. An amazing legacy was born out of his despair and his ability to allow nature to heal his spirit.

Years later, his fifth cousin Franklin D. Roosevelt (FDR) is believed to have contracted polio at thirty-nine years old. Paralyzed from the waist down, swimming soon became his favorite self-prescribed physical therapy to strengthen his upper body. He became an advocate for post-polio recovery efforts. Somehow, he figured out how to stand on his own two feet, literally and figuratively.

FDR became president at the height of the Great Depression and helped a nation regain faith in itself with the New Deal. His famous quote from his first inaugural address, "the only thing we have to fear is… fear itself," spoke to peoples' hearts. He exuded confidence and said that if Congress wouldn't cooperate with his plans to bring financial stability to the country, he would wage war on Congress. He explained to the nation how the banks worked and asked people to have faith in his ability to make those banks solvent again.

He gave his fireside chats to keep the people informed. Together, they were a team, the president and the people. He saved us.

I had never heard these stories about the presidents before. As an American, these men inspire me even more since they are part of our nation's history. They are hopeful, and the lessons they teach are that if life is tough, you should be tougher.

Martin Scorsese, a great director, sums it up. "I mean, if you're scared, if it all seems too daunting, if the machinery of it all seems too big and scary and overwhelming, that's great. You wake up in the morning and you do it anyway. If it seems impossible, that's even better. You do it anyway. And as you go, like I said, remember that amidst all that machinery, you're the one who's going to make the picture. It's just you and the thing that sparked you to make the film. You and the spark—in the end, they're one and the same. You guard that, because it's precious."

When trying to rebuild my life without Thom, I sometimes felt it was too hard to move on. That was a bad attitude. I had to change my focus, stop looking back at what had been and what I no longer had, and start focusing on the future. It was *his* ending, and it was *our* ending, but it was not *my* ending. Now I needed a new beginning.

My attitude was, "Hello, grief. Let's work this thing out." I had to elevate not only my own feelings but the spirits of our beautiful daughters, my happy thoughts.

On an almost daily basis, I recited the Buddhist proverb, "Fall down six times, get up seven." It became my survivor motto.

My yoga teacher, whom I adored, had taken care of not only her dying husband at the end of his life, but also her son. She cared for them pretty much single-handedly. She also kept their bodies in her house for a few days after their deaths, because she believed it would take that long for the soul to disengage from the body. That was not easy either.

Years later, when Thom died, she invited me over to her house for tea and asked if she could read to me some of the lessons her own yoga teacher had written about death. She thought it might help me with my grieving. I remember several things about those Friday afternoon visits.

First, she made me tea, and I got to lie back on the couch in her living room as she read me death lessons from a matching love seat. Being read to was one of the most magical, relaxing experiences I have ever had. It was like she was mothering me. I remember that even more than the lessons she read about.

Second, and more important to me, was what she said during our last afternoon together. "You will not feel it right now, but you have to know… It is still a beautiful life out there." As she looked out her living room windows, her arm majestically swept across everything in her world. "Take it from me."

Third, even more powerful than these words, was the regal way she looked, like there was only beauty out there. That scene looked bleak to me, but the words coming from her gave me hope that I, too, would see the beauty out there one day. I repeated that statement to myself often. "You will not feel it right now, but you have to know… it is still a beautiful life out there."

She spoke the truth. I believed it. And it came true. You can believe it too.

Mining the Lessons

*M*Y FORMER NEIGHBOR GAIL is one of those people who stretches my understanding of life in a good way. It's not so much what happens to her as how she interprets what happens. When presented with a life challenge, she asks herself, *What am I supposed to learn from this?* Everything is a lesson, or as she says, a gift.

Among other things, Gail is a scientist, an occasional cigar smoker, a scotch drinker, a pool player, a teacher, a math whiz, a mother, a wife, a runner, a yoga devotee, and a dog rescuer. One day, she called me from the dog park where she was exercising her two small dogs, Rusty and Freddie.

"Marianne, I need your help! I was just leaving the dog park when two big dogs in a high-speed chase slammed into the back of my right leg and wiped me out. There is a bone sticking out of my lower leg! The ambulance is here now. Which hospital do I tell them to go to?"

I told her which orthopedist and hospital I recommended and what would happen when she got to the emergency room. Later, we talked about how to prepare for surgery to put the bone back in. After she got home and we were able to visit, she asked, "What am I supposed to learn from this?"

We both knew that was coming. After a few tense giggles, we kicked the idea around. Was there something in her life she could not stand (given that now she literally could not stand)? We didn't come up with any significant insight at that time. But here is what I remember about how Gail handled the situation.

Both bones were broken, so her leg was unstable. Therefore, she had to wear what is called "external hardware." Heavy metal rods about the width of a pencil were drilled through the knee and ankle bones, then several longer rods were attached to these shorter ones going up and down both sides of her entire lower leg. The knee was fixed so it could not bend. She could use crutches, but not even touch her toes to the floor. Watching her scoot on her butt, up and down the stairs in her house, is indelibly imprinted in my memory. Her toileting and showering were a two-person affair.

She began to refer to her husband, who worked from home, as "my man." It changed their relationship from two independent working adults to something much more, something which included a caring and trust that had not been a part of their marriage before then.

After a few weeks, Gail was doing floor yoga exercises. I recently saw a picture from those days. She was on her left side, with her opposite leg, the one with the hardware, straight up in the air. She had a smile of accomplishment on her face. She was an inspiration to her orthopedic doctor as well as her family, friends, teachers and students.

When you stop and think about it, Gail had good reasons for grief. She had lost her excellent health, had to have several operations without guaranteed outcomes, became extremely dependent on her husband and friends, had to give up driving, lost her job, and obviously was unable to go for her daily run (her addiction).

Each of these losses is high on the medical stress indices, but added together, they are huge. Yet Gail did not allow herself to feel victimized by them. Each loss presented her with the challenge of negotiating daily life with her severely broken leg.

After that long year, she got the hardware out, started her walking therapy program, moved to Maryland, and eventually began walking and then running again. Easy to say, but oh so hard to do. Oh, and daily yoga. That probably saved her.

Looking back, the lessons were more evident. She said she learned how to ask for and accept help, neither of which she had done before. She learned how to rely on her husband, and he, in turn, became a great caretaker, neither of which they had done before and both of which they enjoyed. They were a team in a new and caring way.

Knowing Gail, there were doubtless many other lessons wrapped up in her story, but the point is her attitude: life teaches us lessons or grants gifts. What she said recently was, "Among other things, it showed me it truly is not the person in the situation, but the person you become in the situation that matters. Oh yeah, and keeping gratitude at the center of everything really helped." She never lost track of that.

Change your attitude from "look at what awful thing has happened to me" to "what can I learn from this challenge?" Then, you can find the lesson or gift in your circumstances. Maybe not right away, but it will wait for you. Open yourself up to the idea that you may have learned a lesson from your own life when you faced a challenge. That shift changes everything, from bathing your brain with chemicals so you don't see yourself as a victim to helping you feel like someone who tried hard and won.

I invite you to join Gail and me in looking for the lessons and gifts in the struggles of life. It is a great way to get beyond the guilt, blame, resentment and other negative side trips that steal your energy. It is all about the outcome, not how it came to you. That part is just life.

My yoga teacher shared that same attitude about life giving you lessons. When I complained about a stretch I found too difficult or uncomfortable, she would say, "That is the one you should do every day. It's the one your body needs to be in balance."

And darn it, she was right. She would then add, like a punctuation mark at the end of a sentence, "Bless your pain. There is your lesson." After hearing that a great number of times, it finally sunk in.

When life is moving right along, it's easy. But when we hit the rough spots, we need to slow down, pay attention, and try to understand what is going on and why. Those are our lessons and gifts.

As I said earlier, the hardest challenges do not mean something is wrong. It means they are the most important ones of all.

The Student Becomes the Teacher

*T*HOSE OF US WHO HAVE MADE IT to our senior years have some wisdom to pass on. Stories are the best way to learn from those who went before us. We first were taught about life from our parents and grandparents. I bet right now you can think of some lessons that have stuck with you.

Our experience taught us what worked and what did not. There were tales of hardships and triumphs, and also scary stories and sacred ones. The oral family history was the basis of our understanding of life.

From our own experiences, we have expanded and changed what we were taught and have incorporated those lessons into the people we have grown to be today. We are more than we were because we have absorbed new ideas, thoughts and feelings—our own as well as those of others.

But we are not done yet.

At this point, we have to transition from life's student to life's teacher. We know our stories will have a lasting impact on our listeners, our young ones. They need to hear our personal stories—not only of our times of enjoyment but also of our challenges and resilience in handling our failures, heartbreaks, traumas and losses. Just by hearing these stories, they can weave them into a strong tapestry, a life of survival, growth and understanding. As mentors and teachers, we can not only support their growth, but insist on it.

Grief is a very important teaching point. It is not taught in school, so it is our responsibility to share what we know. We can teach insights into what grief is, what we can learn from it, how to console someone who is grieving, what it feels like, and how to live with grief.

We can talk about what spirit is, what love is, and what happens when someone dies. We can emphasize the importance of family and community, and our responsibilities to them. We can share stories that teach us how to lead a life based on caring and love.

We all have the opportunity to inspire someone. So, don't hold back. Tell them everything they need to hear and then some. That will instill in your listener the fortitude they need. This is how they can reach their human potential.

The stories I want my children and grandchildren to learn will teach those important lessons, as well as how to be resilient and positive, while remaining undaunted in the face of severe challenges. Above all, I want them to learn how to be grateful for all that life has to give.

Survival Tips

THERE ARE NO SHORTCUTS through grief, no time off for good behavior, no wands to wave the heartache away. Initially, grieving is brutal, but it will not stay that intense. Grief is a process. Over time, the pain softens. One day, you find something—often a small thing—that makes you smile, a reminder that your essence is alive and intact. It is a renewal of faith in yourself, in your spark. Your old self is incorporating your loss into your new self.

A time will come when memories will reflect all the love that you shared. You will not only be grateful for what you had, but look forward to the goodness that is yet to come.

In the meanwhile, you *can* help yourself. Only you hold the key to your inner self. So here are some tips I want to leave with you.

Don't Rush

Take your time. Grieving is a process that unfolds on its own timeline. Remind yourself it's normal to hurt. It just means that someone was very important to you.

It will not always be so painful. The hardest part is often the beginning. Ignore anyone who criticizes your timeline, even yourself. You may have an occasional surge of grief. But it's okay. It won't last.

Focus on Gratitude

Believe it or not, there were some studies done on grievers. Was the pain of loss worth it? Ninety-eight percent responded yes. (That remaining two percent were probably still enraged.)

Despite the pain, they would not have wanted to miss out on all that love and fun.

Maintain a Routine

There is literally a symphony of hormones and vitamins running on a twenty-four-hour clock in your body. You will feel a heck of a lot better if you:

- ∾ go to bed and wake up about the same time each day (give or take an hour).
- ∾ nap no more than thirty minutes (set an alarm).
- ∾ eat something healthy regularly.
- ∾ exercise or walk at least thirty minutes a day.

Limit Decisions

Make important decisions before noon. As the day wears on, your grief brain will begin to fog, and it will be harder to make good choices (or any at all).

If a decision involves money or has life-changing consequences, consult with your smartest friend or financial adviser. You don't want to make any decisions now that you may regret later.

And if you are someone who never paid the bills before and are now challenged to balance your household accounts, get your money-wise friend, bookkeeper or accountant to show you what you need to know. Once you do it a few times, it becomes much easier.

Avoid Using Substances

Alcohol, pills and drugs are not your friends. They are side trips and usually prolong your grief or compound your problems. Often poor decisions are made under the influence that can create even more heartache than what you are already dealing with.

If needed, use the smallest amount for the least amount of time, unless otherwise prescribed by your physician.

It's Okay to Feel Lost

If you can't get out of your own way, if you feel disoriented or lost, try to stay in the moment. Focus on your breathing. Breathe in slowly, count to five, breathe out slowly counting to five again, and then repeat until you settle down.

It also helps to use one of your senses to connect to the natural world. Feel the sun or wind, see the trees or clouds, smell the flowers, or hear the birds or children playing. Senses will help ground you.

If perchance you are lost too long, find a therapist. Ask around. "Know any good therapists?" You will be surprised how many recommendations you get.

Talking to a therapist is not a scary, secret thing. They do not fix you. You fix yourself with their guidance. That is what they are trained to do: to help you get better. Mental health is key to everything.

Take a Grief Break

Pick an amount of time during which you will not allow yourself to grieve. It could be an hour or a day.

During your break, do something simple: go for a walk, sing, play cards or music, dance, watch a movie, cook. Give your grief brain time off.

My favorite break activity is washing the car. By the time you're done, you'll have been outside, concentrated on and accomplished a task, and gotten a clean car.

Listen to Healing Music

Music deserves its own special recognition since it is known to improve brain function on a subconscious level. Even if you have never listened to classical music before, it may help you heal.

I could write more about it, but why don't you google "healing classical music" and give it a try instead? (I do suggest keeping away from popular love songs for now.)

I would suggest starting with Pachebel's Canon in D and even playing it on repeat for a time.

Practice Yoga, Tai Chi, Prayer or Meditation

Yoga and tai chi can be a helpful part of recovering from grief because they are a combination of focused body movements or stretches that require concentration. It is nearly impossible to breathe, focus, stretch and cry at the same time. For someone like me, who has trouble sitting still, it works really well.

Prayer and meditation can be done anywhere in short snatches of time, but they work exceedingly well if you can settle down and focus—or perhaps unfocus; let your mind unwind in grace.

These practices get easier with time. They reward you with inner peace. Do not overlook their power. Each one is mighty. Take your time.

Make Time to Enjoy and Engage

Somehow, in the midst of loss, you realize all the joys you could have celebrated with your loved ones. When I got to this place in my grief, I stocked my fridge with bubbly (prosecco and non-alcoholic drinks).

There is so much to celebrate in life: birthdays, graduations, engagements, concerts, being finished painting the house! The list of struggles and accomplishments goes on—all opportunities to share important moments together. Yippee! Do it!

My intent in all this writing is to connect with you, my fellow griever, and encourage you to keep your chin up. Learn your life lessons with the greatest amount of kindness to yourself and others.

Life is so short and death is so certain. Empower yourself to keep your mind and heart open to all life's beauty and the love that comes your way.

My new self is sending your new self tender loving care.

Embracing the New You

The most beautiful people we have known are those who have known defeat, known suffering, known struggle, known loss, and have found their way out of the depths. These persons have an appreciation, a sensitivity, and an understanding of life that fills them with compassion, gentleness and a deep loving concern. Beautiful people do not just happen.

—Elizabeth Kübler-Ross

O PERSON who has experienced tragedy in their life comes out the same as they were before. Loss teaches you what is most important in life. It teaches you about love and changes your relationship to everyone, including yourself.

Who is this "new you"? It is never too late to be the person you always wanted to be, your best self. If you are rebuilding your inner self after your loss, perhaps that could be your goal now. Be your best self. Match up your new values with the new and improved you that death has created.

What do you want to bring to this life? What do you stand for? The answers to these questions are your "gifts" from loss. There are no lightning bolts or neon signs saying where to go or what to do, but you probably feel a connectedness to your heart and spirit that was not there before. It may be subtle. Listen for those answers. If you can't hear them at first, then wait. They will become more obvious as the shock of your loss wears off. The answers lie inside of you. They are your keys to understanding who you are now.

There are other gifts that grief may leave with you. One is what I call "anticipatory grief" and the other is "preparatory grief." The first stems from fear, the other from learning how to mitigate the pain of a future loss.

People who have suffered a traumatic loss experience unique fears about losing anyone else. This aspect of grief is triggered when your new loved one fills the space someone else once held in your life. Here are a couple of examples.

When Thom and I were driving to Los Angeles to pick out our wedding rings, I had a full blown panic attack. We had to stop the car so I could get out and catch my breath. It came as a surprise to me, but not to Thom (the death and dying therapist).

"Well, honey… We are doing the same thing that you and Kerry were going to do the day he died, picking out our wedding rings. I think it's kind of normal that you would have some kind of reaction."

Sometimes I think if I didn't have Thom there explaining the events in my life while I was enmeshed in them, I would have thought I was just crazy. Looking back now, it seems more obvious to me what was going on in my mind and body.

A few years ago, Gene and I were riding in the back seat of my sister's car, up the mountain, to where she was going to marry us. Gene took the wide-eyed expression on my face to mean I was feeling the same excitement he was. On the contrary, I was talking myself down from a near panic attack.

Thoughts flew through my mind as quickly as a shuffling deck of cards. What was I doing? Was I setting myself up for yet another heartbreak? Why am I worrying that he will die before me? I could die before him. Would I actually let the pain of my past rob me of the joy of my future? There are no guarantees going forward.

I didn't expect these prenuptial jitters but, by the time we got to the top of the mountain, I was able to let go of worrying about my future, feeling triggered by my past. Instead, I stayed in the bliss of committing to love a new partner. Gene and I now both laugh at the re-telling of this story. It feels good to be able to laugh at yourself sometimes.

These examples demonstrate how a shocking loss sets up alerts in your brain. Your body and mind remember emotional pain. When your caution signal lights up, reminding you that this situation caused pain before, tell yourself "That was then, and this is now." There is a difference. You understand now that pain doesn't mean an experience was wrong or must be avoided in the future, only that it was really important to you and provided a difficult learning opportunity.

You have incorporated many of these lessons into your understanding of life, and you are simply adjusting. It's like the old GPS. When you went off the planned route, a gentle voice would say, "Recalculating." You are doing the same, incorporating what you've learned and moving on.

Shortly after Gene and I got married, we made up our "what if..." plan. Most likely one of us would die before the other. Each of us having been through it before, we wanted our death to be easier for the one left behind. Knowing each other's wishes in advance could help. We also had our wills drawn up. Although the conversations about "if you die first or if I die first" weren't easy, the feeling of being prepared as much as possible was essential. You don't want to be left wondering what to do when you have a grieving brain. After we accomplished our what-if plans, we went out to dinner and celebrated.

These decisions were prompted by preparatory grief in the hopes of making the situation easier for each of us when the time came. (Hopefully, a very long time from now!)

One of the things our girls talk about off and on are the things they would like us to leave them when we die. They have seen the struggles people have when dealing with possessions left behind after their grandparents, uncles and friends died. There are a few things that have significant meaning to each of the girls that we have earmarked for them because we know it will make their life easier or more meaningful. Hopefully, it will lessen the burden of their grief. If you flip over artwork in our house, you may see one of my daughters' names on it. That's theirs when Gene and I are gone.

The loss you've suffered has taught you many things. But don't let fear or anticipatory grief hold you back from embracing life again. Let preparatory grief guide you to help lessen the pain of a future loss and allow you to fearlessly welcome the love in your life.

The way ahead is sprinkled with hope, awareness, forgiveness, understanding and challenges, along with whispers of "you can do it." Those of us who have gone before will leave a secret trail of connectedness for you to follow so you, too, can be a survivor.

> Knock down your walls.
>> *Open your heart.*
> You have power in your life.
>> *You will feel it more now.*
> Look for it.
>> *It is waiting there.*
> Use it.
>> *You can do it.*

The phoenix is a mythical bird of great beauty that burns itself on a funeral pyre to rise again from the ashes in the freshness of youth, to live on through another lifetime.

You will be that phoenix, who rises from the ashes whole and renewed from grief. You will soar above it all.

Part VI. Kids and Grief

Talking to Children

*T*HE FACT THAT THERE ARE CHILDREN in families where a parent, sibling or close family member dies is no surprise. What *is* unbelievable is when no one talks to the children about it. That is devastating to a young soul. What a child imagines is often worse than the reality of death.

But what do you say to a child? How do you help a young person grieve? Let's face it. Most people do not know what to say to another adult. Talking to a child about death can be even more challenging.

Children process grief more easily in small bits. Here are nine essential points for communicating about death with children.

1. **Children feel grief too.**
   They are way more intuitive than we give them credit for. When you are upset, they know it. They can feel not only lost, scared and alone but also invisible. If you

think you are protecting them or hope to avoid upsetting them by not talking about the death of someone they love, think again. It sends the wrong message, implying that they do not count or should not be feeling the way they are.

2. **Use the words "died" and "dead."**

   Young children understand words literally. Saying someone "left us" means they can come back. Saying they are "going to sleep" means they can wake up. Be clear. State that the loved one who died cannot come back. Their body cannot see, breathe or talk.

3. **Be honest, but keep it simple.**

   If it's suicide, say it.

   "Your sister had an illness in her brain that made her very depressed. It caused her to think that living with this mental illness was unbearable, so she chose to end her life by taking too many pills, which made her body stop working."

   If it's an accident, say it.

   "Mom was in a car accident. The car slid on the ice and hit a tree. She died from injuries that made it impossible for her to breathe anymore."

   If it's murder, say it.

   "Your brother was in a nightclub dancing and having fun when he was killed by a man with a gun. This man had crazy thoughts and shot a lot of people. It is impossible to understand. I know it's hard for you. It's hard for me too."

4. **Reassure them that they could not have changed or caused what happened.**

   Children often feel guilty about something they did wrong and draw a connection between that and why a person died. They can even feel it was their fault that the person died. It is imperative they know their thoughts or actions had no effect on their loved one's death. They are not being punished for bad behavior. (This is the same advice given to children during a divorce.)

5. **Talk about feelings—yours and theirs—even if you are uncomfortable.**

   Kids understand the four basic emotions: happy, sad, angry and scared. You can share these feelings with them.

   ∽ "I am sad because…"

   ∽ "How do you feel right now?"

   ∽ "Do you ever feel scared like me?"

   These questions can begin a conversation about feelings. You may be surprised by what they are really thinking. And the more real you can be with them, the healthier their adjustment to the loss. Just keep your sharing brief. And that leads into my next point.

6. **Let them talk.**

   The hardest and most important part is being patient. Let the child ask their questions. Those questions tell you where they are in their thinking and where you need to go with your conversation. Sometimes, things are said at school or on the radio or on TV that can be misconstrued by a young listener. If something bothers them, they need to be able to bring it up. Ask an open-ended question, like "How are you doing?"

7. **Anger is part of grief.**

   If your life is never going to be the same, it can make you angry. Kids feel that way too. This anger needs a healthy outlet. Some children find it easiest to express their feelings through activities like drawing, writing, doll/puppet play, punching a pillow or screaming. It has to get out.

8. **There is no timeline for grief.**

   Grieving usually takes a lot longer than we want. Just because your children can play and run around with their friends does not mean they are fine.

9. **Teach them death cannot break their spirit.**

   They will survive, thrive and be happy again, even if it does not feel that way at first. Hold out hope at all times. Through loss, we can learn the lessons of resilience and gratitude for who we are and what we have. Families and communities need to stick together. This interconnectedness teaches children we are all affected by what happens to each other. Connection builds trust. Through that connectedness, children will feel the love that surrounds them. They get the message: Love soothes heartache. Life will go on. They will be okay.

Some of these ideas came from an article written by my colleague Sharon Diaz for a local magazine, while others developed over my years in practice.

Sharon is a psychotherapist who works with families. Years after dealing with her young, grieving niece and nephew, she has focused on helping kids and their families work through their own grief. As a result, she has a great understanding of what works best with young children.

Remember, you are human. If your children are grieving, then you most likely are too. Be gentle with yourself. You will probably make some mistakes along the way. Forgive yourself. Let it go. If you said something to your child that was wrong, just admit it—say it was wrong and that you are sorry, and ask for forgiveness.

In my experience, children are much quicker to forgive than adults. Maybe we can learn the grace of forgiveness from them.

Guilty Goodbyes

*W*HEN THEIR DAD DIED, Justine was eight years old and Caitlin was thirteen. The five years between my daughters' ages made all the difference in how they grieved. Looking back, I missed some of their cues since I was mired in grief too.

Caitlin was a busy high school freshman at a college preparatory school. When she wasn't in class, she hung out with friends, like most teens do.

Justine was in third grade, always either in the horse barn or at home. She was often on an emotional roller coaster—sometimes quiet and sensitive, other times angry and obnoxious. Being stuck at home with her dying father and stressed-out mother probably had something to do with that. Fortunately, she was always verbal, so when she acted up I could ask her what was going on and she would let me know.

One day, while driving Justine to the horse barn, we stopped at our mailbox at the top of the driveway. She was quiet, but I could see her face. Her thick black hair was pulled back in a low ponytail so her riding helmet would fit. She was chewing on her lower lip and picking at her nails. I could see a storm brewing in that beautiful head of hers.

I waited and looked at her with raised eyebrows in that mom way, asking, "What's up?"

"Mom, I think I might have to talk to somebody."

"Okay, honey. I am listening."

"No, Mom. I mean a professional. Like Dad, but not Dad."

"Oh, I see. Something kinda private?" I was lost.

She thought while biting her nails. "Yeah, it's about Dad."

"The kind of thing that really bothers you?" I was still searching for the cause of her stress.

She nodded, and the heaviness of her thoughts permeated the car.

"Well, we can make that happen. Sure." My mind raced along, trying to figure out what was going on in her head. Okay, it was about her dad, who was dying. I got that. "Sometimes, I have thoughts about Dad that I don't always talk to him about."

"You do?"

"Sure. With him and the cancer, there are some scary things to think about."

Justine's jaw tensed, and she stared out the windshield, deep in thought.

"What I'm scared about are the bad thoughts," she said.

"Bad thoughts?" Holy cow! What was she thinking?

"Yeah…" She stopped talking.

"Like what, honey?" I was trying to tease out the crux of the problem.

"Well… Sometimes, I just want him to die so we can have a life again. But then I feel so bad that I want my dad dead. I am a bad person." She deflated like a punctured balloon. Her silent tears fell, refusing to be contained any longer. Justine was processing her dad's impending death, but I had no idea she had been feeling so badly about herself.

"Oh, sweetheart…" I took her hands and kissed them, as she looked at me through her tears.

"Justine, my love, I want to tell you a secret. Sometimes, I have those bad thoughts too."

My daughter's eyebrows flew up as she looked at my face.

"I want Dad to die so it will be over, so I can stop spending every day and every night sharing a bedroom with a dying man who is not going to get better."

Justine took a deep breath.

"So you and Caitlin and Sarah and I can get on with life, even if it is a life without Dad."

"That's *it*, Mom. That's what I wanted to talk to someone about." The catch in her throat told me this had been bothering her for a while.

"Oh, honey. You are not bad. Even those thoughts are not so bad. You just want it to be over. I get it. I really do." She was just a kid. These were intense feelings, even for me!

"What happens to me when I think that way is I feel bad about wanting Dad dead, but really I just want the dying over. We already know he's not going to beat this cancer. He is going to die. It's just a matter of when."

"Right," Justine responded.

Now I could see her calm down. Like lancing a boil, the worst was out and now there would be less pain and more healing.

More deep breaths.

I continued. "I feel that way too, only I was afraid to tell anyone because it sounds so weird. Maybe whoever I told wouldn't really get it. I have just been living with that awful secret inside me." She had to know she was not alone.

"Wow! So you feel that way too, Mom?"

"I sure do. Sometimes it just makes me so pissed off, I don't know what to do."

The tears had stopped. She was not chewing her nails now, and her face was more relaxed. The tension in the car, like the feeling of breathing in smog, had lifted.

"But actually, after talking to you, Justine, I feel a lot better. How about you?" I wanted her to know the value of talking it through.

"Mom"—she exhaled, and everything relaxed—"you have no idea."

Getting a child to talk about their feelings is far from easy, but it is essential. You can dispel their misconceptions, reduce their guilt, and help them feel supported. When those things happen, grieving is so much less complicated.

Laughter is the Best Medicine

*A*T THE END OF MY MOTHER'S LIFE, when she couldn't get out of bed anymore, I would give her a bed bath. One day, with my mother's consent, Caitlin and Justine assisted "to make Nana feel better." To this day, we all remember...

With her arm out, I washed and rinsed, Caitlin dried, and Justine massaged in the body lotion. And so it went with each arm and leg. The sighs and tiny moans of pleasure from their grandmother were something we all still treasure.

Of course, for some reason, humor always seems to be a part of everything my family does. So, when my staid, strict mother, who believed all dogs were "outside dogs," invited Angeline, our white fluffy dog, onto her bed, we were shocked.

"Mom!" I said. "I can't believe you would allow a dog to get on your bed." At this point, Angeline decided the best place for her was on the pillow just on top of my mother's head, with her front paws hanging down one side of Mom's head and her rear paws dangling down the other.

Angeline settled in like she was following a script from a movie. The girls and I looked at Angeline, now a "dog hat" on my dying mother's head. Caitlin, Justine and I couldn't stop giggling and snickering. It's like laughing in church—you know you shouldn't be doing it, but that makes it impossible to stop.

When my mother asked why we were laughing, I told her about her dog hat. She replied, completely deadpan, "Well, you have me in a weakened condition."

That made the three of us laugh even harder while my mother simply smiled.

As I reflect on this experience, I see several important lessons.

- ∾ Death is an opportunity for togetherness.
- ∾ Death allows you to break the rules of "good behavior."
- ∾ My mom was not left to die alone in her room.
- ∾ My children got to make their dying grandmother feel better.
- ∾ Since my children got to experience dying firsthand, it was not so scary after all.
- ∾ When it came time for their father to die, my children had a framework for how it went.
- ∾ None of my mother's other grandchildren had an experience like this, and some of them felt cheated out of closure about her death.

∾ We have a humorous story of death that we
  all enjoy.

∾ Humor is powerful.

Grief is not usually a feeling associated with humor, but as time wears down the sharp, painful edges of grieving, a funny story like this gives it a slightly different perspective and provides a break from all the sobriety.

Laughter provides its own magic.

Parting Words

*Y*OUR LOSS TEACHES YOU not only that life is short, but that it is precious. What is the meaning of my life? What do I want to bring to the time I have left? Perhaps you already know the answers to these questions, but the answers are more pertinent now because of who and what you lost. Your loss is your loved one's wake-up gift to you. Now is the time to do whatever crazy good you can in the world. Don't hold back. Let your love loose.

So many people need help. Look around and you will see it. Give without expectation of return to someone you love, your family, your community, or a stranger in need. There is great power in the person who receives, but also in the person who gives.

Now you know. Grief has given you the power of understanding. It is precious, and so are you.

To Live Again

Like the rock of Gibraltar, my anger was massive,
undeniable and immutable.

Anger was my enemy. Yet my heart was encased in it.
My mind, at some time, decided it was time to dismantle it.

At the ocean, I stood where the water washed over my feet.
With each lap of a wave, the tide drew out a bit of anger, sending
     it out into the deep.

Looking over the vast blue sky, I cast my angry thoughts into
     the wind,
which blew it to pieces, scattering its dust over the universe.

On the earth, I flung anger like fertilizer in my garden,
rearranging its molecules to feed my dahlias, cosmos and zinnias.

In the fire, I burned up my anger in a white-hot blaze
until that massive pile of broken hopes and dreams became ash.

Anger would release its hold on me.
I would move forward without the bloody wounds.

They would heal. Scarred, I would move forward.
I would live again.

I would.
I willed it to be so.

—Marianne Bette

Thank you for reading *Living with a Grieving Heart*.
If you've enjoyed reading this book, please leave a review
on your favorite review site. It helps me reach more
readers who may benefit from encouragement and
support as they go through their own grieving process.

Read on for a peek at Marianne and Thom's story.

Excerpt from
Living with a Dead Man

Marianne Bette, MD

Diagnosis

"Cancer changes everything. Forever and forever."
– Marty Ludorf, with three close family
members with breast cancer

*S*ITTING IN AN ONCOLOGIST'S WAITING ROOM is one of life's more sobering experiences. The first thing that hit me was that I was there, not as a doctor, but as a cancer patient's wife.

Cancer patient.

Those two words are one big mouthful.

Kert's waiting room was rather unimaginative. The room was lined on either side with chairs. Each one, I noted, had arm rests to help frail people to get up. Occasional end tables were covered with old magazines. Boxed fluorescent lighting shone from the ceiling.

The receptionist sat behind a window busily working on a computer. When she told us to have a seat, Thom and

I each grabbed a magazine and headed to the far end of the waiting room.

We were sitting near a large fake plant that was supposed to look like ornamental grass. I was thinking that if it was real it might be able to give some sort of comfort to the people around it. But where would it get its light? Were there any nurturing souls there that would care for it? I guessed a plastic plant was better than no plant or worse yet a dead one. Maybe someday I would talk to Kert about this.

As I sat with an outdated issue of People Magazine in my lap, I looked around the room with my doctor-mind at work.

Across from us was an older couple sitting side-by-side, quietly reading.

He looked like an average healthy 70-year-old man. He had mostly white to gray hair, glasses, tanned skin, mildly arthritic hands, a beige zipper jacket, chinos and deck shoes.

His wife (I assumed) had one of those head wrap scarves on her head. She had no hair sticking out like you would expect at the temples or nape of her neck and she was striking in her paleness. Her face was white, her hands were white, and her neck was white. Anemia, I diagnosed. Doubtless, a result of the chemo. Color and *joie de vivre* are the first to go. She was dressed for winter, even though it was mid-May.

Maybe she is going to get a unit of blood today, I thought. I hoped so because she would look and feel a lot better then Now, she looked as if she was being erased.

To their right was another couple, obviously mother and daughter. The mother looked quite similar to the pale lady except she was older and more feeble. She seemed as if she had lost her way. She was confused and undone in her manner, he:

speech and her dress, and she looked like she had just rolled out of bed.

The daughter sat next to her with a clipboard on her lap. It had a number of papers on it, a list of questions and lab results. She seemed irritated with her mother. I wondered what their relationship was usually like. What happened to make her so out of sorts? Is her mother getting worse? Is the mother leaning too heavily on the daughter? Is she the caretaker? Maybe the daughter is getting burned out herself?

On our side of the room were two women. One had very short hair—growing in after chemo, or so it seemed. She actually looked pretty good. Although I couldn't hear what they were saying, the conversation seemed animated and she gave off this attitude like, "I survived the chemo and beat the cancer, and I am here to get the good news."

Boy, I sure hope so. Her companion had a hopeful look too. Who is she? The sister? They don't look alike… maybe her partner or best friend.

Which cancer did she beat? Breast cancer, I assume. *Go, girl. Someone's got to win sometime.*

Another patient entered the waiting room holding a stainless steel bowl (known as a "throw-up pan" at our house). They go right in. No waiting room time for them, thank goodness.

At the other end of the waiting room, there was a middle-aged man reading by himself. He was probably picking someone up after their chemo. He would be the driver.

There was an empty chair between him and the next man who also looked pretty healthy. He was about 65 and had all his hair, his color was good and his face looked bright. I wondered how he fit in here, in the oncologist's waiting room.

As I scanned his clothes, I saw it. The little plastic tubing sticking out of the end of his red plaid sleeve. Yep, him too. He was here for chemo. He was probably just starting since he looked so good. It usually takes two or three rounds before hair falls out and anemia sets in.

A round middle-aged lady in scrubs called our names, interrupting my doctoral review of the waiting room and bringing me back to my own reality. "The doctor is running behind, but you can sit and wait in his office."

I felt as if a temporary reprieve had been granted.

The assistant gave us the office tour. Immediately inside the door on the right was the blood drawing room. On the left was the scale, just like in my office, but it had a completely different significance in an oncologist's office where cancer patients struggle to maintain their weight.

As we turned right down the hallway to Kert's office, we passed by a large open room with lots of windows. It was filled with eight or ten La-Z-Boy recliners. Half of the seats were occupied by people attached by clear plastic tubing to bags hung on IV poles.

Some people were watching television. Others were sleeping under colorful hand-crocheted blankets like my grandmother made. One pale man was reclining with his eyes closed and earphones plugged in. I wondered if listening to classical music would reduce the nausea that often goes along with the chemo.

"This is our chemo room," the assistant said proudly. "People usually stay here for a few hours. They can read or sleep or even bring in their own DVDs to watch."

She said it cheerfully, like they were great choices. My doctor head was noting how it all worked, but my wife head was wondering how my husband will feel, sitting there watching TV in a room-full of people he doesn't know, who are all getting poison pumped into their veins that makes them feel like throwing up.

We waited in Kert's office, walking around, looking at his pictures and diplomas. We were way too nervous to sit. Soon, Kert came bustling in and apologized for being late, as if he hadn't squeezed us into his already full schedule. His small frame and stature belied the articulate, insightful and empathetic giant I know him to be.

In his office, he had that professional look and attitude that lets you know he means business—quite a different view from the impish, playful Kert that my call partner, Craig, and I get together with for the occasional drink on a Friday night. In that one hour of unwinding, we would catch up on each other's kids, travels and good books recently read.

I knew from those conversations that Kert loves to cycle, cook and spend time with his wife, with whom he is madly in love even after 25 years of marriage. But that was not the man I saw before me. We were here to see the doctor, not the friend I know and love.

He pulled the two chairs from in front of his desk and placed them side-by-side in the middle of the room. Then he rolled his desk chair around to face the two chairs.

"Please sit down," he said gesturing for Thom and me to sit facing him.

"I came in early this morning and reviewed your scans myself. Then I went over them with the neuroradiologist I respect the most. I also spoke with the interventional radiologist about what has to happen next. But before I go into all this, Thom can you tell me exactly what happened to you yesterday?"

Kert has this incredible ability to focus on you in a way that lets you know you have his total concentration. As Thom related his story, Kert never took his eyes off Thom. Clearly, I was not the focus.

My doctor head was happy that a connection was being established between the doctor and patient, not the patient's doctor-spouse.

When Thom was finished, Kert summarized the situation. "This looks like a small lung cancer in the left lung. There is also a spot in the left brain. In order to know how best to treat it, we need a piece of tissue under the microscope to know exactly which type of cancer it is. The easiest area to get a piece of is the lung, that's why I spoke to the interventional radiologist. He feels he could get into the cancer with a small needle right from the outside of your chest. He could do this in the x-ray department, after numbing you up of course, and then assuming you are stable you could go home right after that. Once we get the report back, we will plan our treatment."

Lots of questions went back and forth about chemotherapy, surgery and radiation. Then Kert set up the lung biopsy and he made us an appointment with the neurosurgeon to talk about removing the tumor in Thom's head.

At the end, Kert looked at me and asked tenderly, "And how are you doing, Marianne?"

Those few words and that caring look on Kert's face unleashed the floodgates. I looked from Kert to Thom as I became blinded by my tears. Kert was clearly talking to me as his friend, not a colleague and not a patient's wife.

"This is all my fault," I began. "I'm the one who wanted to move back here with my whole crazy family. We built this big house that just seemed to grow and grow until it took us to near bankruptcy. The general contractors were my brother and my nephew. We loved them, but there were a lot of problems and eventually Thom had to fire them and take over the job himself. It had a terrible affect on him. He started drinking to cope. And then he just kept on drinking."

[You see, I had a theory about cancer. Our bodies make cancer cells all the time and usually our immune system detects those cells and destroys them. Why cancer cells sneak under the radar and actually form a tumor no one knows for sure, but I had long held the theory that stress had something to do with immobilizing the immune system. And if stress had caused Thom's cancer, then I was guilty.]

I paused to look at Kert, who clearly was trying to grasp what I was saying. "We worked through all that, but I know it was all that stress, all that awful stress, that allowed this cancer to happen."

Wiping my eyes as I turned to look at Thom, I apologized. "I'm so sorry, honey. I am sorry we moved here. I know you did it for me and the girls, but now I wish you hadn't. If we had moved somewhere else, this never would have happened to you."

As I sobbed into my tissues, Thom reached out and took my hand and caressed it. "Or," he began, "it could be thirty years of smoking!"

I looked up, startled. He was actually smirking at me! I almost laughed in response, but in that exact moment, I realized that he was right. It wasn't the move to Connecticut or, at any rate, if it was it only had a minor effect compared to the years he had poisoned himself with cigarettes.

I went from tears to rage in one second flat. He had done this to himself. He had done it to me. He had done it to the girls. I turned on him so fast his head must have been spinning.

"Why? Why did you do that? Why did you keep smoking?" I demanded an answer.

Kert, who I had forgotten about for the moment, jumped in. "Marianne, you did not cause your husband's cancer. And Thom certainly didn't intend to get cancer. Come on now, let's focus on how to get out of this mess and see what needs to be done next."

The tirade stopped. For now.

Living with a Dead Man
is available at emeraldlakebooks.com/LWDM.

Author's Note

*F*OR THOSE OF YOU who know me personally or have read my earlier book, I thought I would offer a quick update on the girls, at least as of early 2022.

Sarah remarried four years ago to a chef, who is a perfect match for her. They opened a restaurant, Peasant Feast, in Solvang, California, at the beginning of the COVID-19 shutdown! Although they didn't have a single diner eat inside their restaurant their first year in business, they were winning awards and keeping their heads above water, often with just takeout!

Caitlin and Justine both now live in North Carolina, about three hours apart. Caitlin is a family physician and emergency room doctor in a small town in the Blue Ridge Mountains, north of Asheville. She and her partner from residency have started a practice on a Direct Primary Care model. They join with young family doctors across the country to revolutionize modern medicine, yet it harks back to what us old-time family docs did forty years ago. It warms my heart to know this type of doctoring can still happen, free from insurance restrictions.

Her tales of her patient relationships are doubly precious to me because my pride in her success is matched by my delight at having a unique, shared life experience: mother/daughter and doctor. Bliss!

Justine owns an animal rescue farm, also in the Blue Ridge Mountains—in her case, near Tennessee. Her Cedar Cliff Sanctuary has horses, chickens, rabbits, a pig, and too many cats and dogs to count. Most recently, she has adopted a wolf puppy, a squirrel with seizures, a goat struck by lightning, and a sugar glider—it glides like a flying squirrel and is native to North Carolina. This glider is the widow of a bonded pair. Justine bonded with the animal while it was still grieving, and it has since flourished.

Previously, she was a horse whisperer. Now, she is an all-round animal whisperer. She does all kinds of work to keep her farm and feed her animals. She too is amazing.

My three girls are beautiful, both inside and out. These women have found their passions in life, and for that reason, are all genuinely happy despite the usual day-to-day struggles. Life has moved on for all of us.

More Help

NPR (National Public Radio) has several great podcasts on grief, which you can google.

There are also plenty of websites that can help coordinate the efforts of friends and family to support a grieving loved one. Two that I'm familiar with include mealtrain.com and carecalendar.com.

And here are some other helpful reading materials.

Bette, Marianne. *Living with a Dead Man*. Emerald Lake Books, 2016.

Birenbaum, Steven. "How to Hold a Virtual Memorial Service," *New York Times* (1/14/21). emeraldlakebooks.com/virtualfuneral. Last accessed: May 20, 2022.

Cappabianca, Geralyn. *Memoirs of a Hospital Chaplin: I Stand Near the Door*. Createspace, 2015.

Sood, Amit. "A Very Happy Brain," MayoClinic.org. emerald-lakebooks.com/happybrain. Last accessed: May 20, 2022.

Warner, Jan. *Grief Day by Day: Simple Practices and Daily Guidance for Living With Loss.* Althea Press, 2018.

Weller, Francis. *The Wild Edge of Sorrow. Rituals of Renewal and the Sacred Work of Grief.* North Atlantic Books, 2015.

Acknowledgments

I HAVE OFTEN SEEN the acknowledgments authors write but never fully understood them until now. I will speak from my experience with my second book.

A book takes more creative talent than I appreciated, not only from the author but from the editor. Tara and her team, but especially Tara herself, has a gift that puts the polish on the story. She is the editor extraordinaire. Whenever I would get sidetracked by the story, she would remind me how the reader would see it. Since my purpose in writing this book was to help you with your own grief, learning how to see my stories from the reader's point of view and tease out the lessons from them for you was very significant.

In the hours we have spent together crafting these stories for you, we have been able to share our own experiences in loss and heartbreak as well as grief. Together we have tried to include the most important elements that we believe need to be covered. Perhaps other editors have shared this unique bond that leads to trust and friendship. That I don't know. I only know this book would not be what it is without her talent and now we have a friendship established on common experiences we have shared.

What could have been a monumental task for me became a collaborative effort that I actually looked forward to. Tara and her team are aces. And I am so glad she has consented to stick with me and my atrocious spelling and poor grammar with yet another book. I learned so much with this one, so I am hoping the next one will be a bit easier. (Thank God for spell-check!)

My friends were also essential in their support and encouragement while I wrote this book. Sometimes with dinner conversations, walks, reading or just plain listening. These individuals include Deborah Bette, Kathleen Lord and Lisa V. Keller, as well as my husband Gene. Thank you, my dears.

The people who were willing to read and endorse my book are those who I admire for their work in our related fields. Their feedback is essential.

Equally important are the wonderful friends and patients who were willing to share their heart and soul with me regarding their own stories.

All these people have enriched my life in ways that mere words could not express.

Everyone has filled me with a type of love that remains undefined.

Thank you again and again.

About the Author

ARIANNE BETTE is a retired family physician from Southbury, Connecticut, the town where she was born and raised and still currently lives.

After forty years in family medicine, she's enjoying her retirement and getting to spend time with her second husband, Gene. The two of them have a truck camper in which they have traveled around the United States, including driving to Alaska and back. (One of their favorite travel destinations.) They share a trusty rescue dog named Buttons, who is their constant companion and she loves camping too.

Marianne has three daughters she's very proud of. Her oldest daughter Sarah lives in southern California with her family. While her other two daughters, Caitlin and Justine, both live in North Carolina.

A consummate gardener and home chef, Marianne has also begun work on a third book. This one includes the inspiring stories of some of her former patients.

Marianne loves to connect with her readers on Instagram (@bettemarianne) and invites you to follow her there.

If you're interested in having Marianne come speak to your group or organization, either online or in person, you can contact her at emeraldlakebooks.com/bette.

For more great books, please visit us at
emeraldlakebooks.com.

Made in the USA
Las Vegas, NV
22 August 2023

76423883R00125